The Nature of War

The Nature

# of War

John Keegan &
Joseph Darracott

A Jonathan-James Book

Holt, Rinehart and Winston
New York

Published by Holt, Rinehart and Winston,
383 Madison Ave., New York,
N.Y. 10017

Library of Congress Cataloging in Publication Data

Keegan, John, 1934-
   The nature of war.

   1. War. I. Darracott, Joseph, joint author.
II. Title.
U21.2.K4 1981   355'.02   80-23979
ISBN 0-03-057777-2

First Edition

Created and produced by
Jonathan-James Books
225 Duncan Mill Road
Don Mills, Ontario
Canada, M3B 1Z3

Editor: Patrick Crean
Project editors: David Homel, Barbara Purchase
Picture researcher: Elly Beintema
Designer: Maher & Murtagh

Printed in Hong Kong
10 9 8 7 6 5 4 3 2 1

To the vision of peace

Table of Contents

Introduction

War is an activity that modern Western man prefers to banish to the remotest corner of his consciousness. Violence is blessedly absent from his everyday world of work and family, and such images of fighting as he receives come to him from distant places through television or newspapers. For those with a taste for the subject, movies and books provide a version of war that may excite their interest and sense of pity, but its substance touches them not at all. Even the realist can therefore convince himself that warfare has become outmoded and alien to his way of life. The fact of war his reason cannot deny; its potential to disrupt the settled order of things his emotions will not admit.

In any age before the present, only a dreamer or an innocent would have possessed an outlook so determinedly optimistic. Not that the past didn't know episodes of something like universal peace, at least within the boundaries of civilization: for much of the second and third centuries the Roman Empire was untroubled by war; and during the nineteenth century the British, by ignoring their imperial campaigns and treating the Crimean war as an aberration, persuaded themselves that they had entered a perpetually pacific era. But intervals such as these, which in any case look more peaceful at a distance than under close scrutiny, are islands in a vast ocean of storms. No part of the earth's surface on which men live or travel has not been fought over at some time or other. Some spots, like Adrianople in European Turkey and Antioch in Syria, have been fought over time and again. Armies are attracted to such places for "strategic" reasons, meaning that possession or control of the area is desirable usually because it stands at points of communication between one productive region and another. It might be suggested then that the prevalence and frequency of war arise out of one group's desire or need to prey upon the land or wealth of another. What we know of the earliest warfare endorses this view, and it is further borne out in our own world where the correlation between deprivation and aggression is undeniable. Yet want does not sufficiently explain why we engage in battle. The richest and most powerful states are frequently the most warlike, whereas the poor are often too weak to resist even a direct threat to their independence. War serves many purposes: revenge, remonstrance, religion and ideology, as well as acquistiveness and pre-emption. For some societies it is a last resort undertaken with reluctance and distaste; for others it shapes and informs their whole character and is embarked upon in anticipation of glory and triumph. But no known society, however high-minded, has been able to banish war from its dealings with others; nor, because the urges that underlie warfare are individual as well as collective, has a society been able to base itself on any but an ultimately military foundation.

If any individual member of a society might be expected to show immunity to warlike impulses, it would be the artist. Material considerations play a subordinate role in his motivation, and the requirements of his personal life turn on a physical freedom and liberty of action antipathetic to military discipline and obedience. And yet the action and ethos of warfare undoubtedly exert a most powerful fascination on the artistic imagination. Music, least concrete of the arts, is least touched by it. But poets, writers, sculptors and painters have returned to it time and again. Its universality as a literary subject is much explored. Although its recurrence in pictorial art, particularly in painting, has been much less recognized and little studied, some of our earliest graphic images, from Pharaonic Egypt and Assyria, are of war. In fact, several of the oldest surviving paintings on earth – twelve-thousand-year-old paintings from the caves of the Pyrenees – show men with weapons in their hands. Next to biblical motifs, war was the main concern of mediaeval art. And despite the move toward portraiture and landscape in the Renaissance, high European art dwells on the theme of humanistic man as warrior and conqueror. Sometimes the choice of a military subject was dictated by the artist's being an employee of an imperial court, as was Velasquez; sometimes it was commissioned, as by the Duke of Bavaria from Altdorfer (see *The Battle of Issus*); and sometimes it seems to have established a hold on the artist's imagination, impelling him to return to it in one picture after another, as with Wouwermans and in the later work of Goya. The Neo-classical movement, which stimulated the study of Greek and Roman history and legend, inevitably produced much war art, and the coincidence of this movement with the French Revolution and Napoleonic conflicts encouraged the treatment of contemporary military themes in the fashionable heroic style. For different though emotionally cognate reasons, the Romantics were equally drawn to war. Delacroix therefore appears as military an artist as David. And the fashion for explicitly "historical" painting, which dominated Salon painting in the second half of the nineteenth century, expressed itself in a flood of battle pictures.

By a parallel movement, the late 1800s saw the appearance of a school of specifically military artists who, together with the new breed of war correspondents, were received on a formal footing by campaigning armies and accorded facilities to depict events, either for rapid circulation through illustrated newspapers using novel repro-graphic processes or for the creation of official works of art for display in public museums. The value of the right sort of art for propaganda purposes had been recognized by the Medici and energetically sponsored by a succession of conquering kings and emperors, from Charles V to Napoleon. In the aggressively nationalistic atmosphere of late nineteenth- and early twentieth-century Europe, the artist became one of the most flattered and influential political agents of every great sovereign state. During the two world wars, the governments of all the combatants commissioned practising artists to work at the front and record their visions of the scene. In the authoritarian states, the results were dreary documents, bereft of inspiration. In the democracies, where individuality was not limited or repressed, some war art managed to achieve a genuine quality of energy and truth.

Whatever its origins and impetus, the depiction of the warrior and his world is an important, even if neglected, element of the artistic vision. This book assembles examples of that art in its manifold variety, from the recruiting and training of soldiers and their departure on campaign, through the field maneuvers, sieges and battles, to the tending of the wounded and burying of the dead. Its purpose is to reveal something of a phenomenon which, however repugnant to all that is sensitive and generous in human nature, is nevertheless universal in the life of mankind.

The
Nature of War

I
Peace & Prelude

Jacob van Ruisdael,
View Towards Haarlem.

Ring out the old, ring in the new

Ring out the false, ring in the true.

Ring out false pride in place and blood,
The civic slander and the spite;
Ring in the love of truth and right,
Ring in the common love of good.

Ring out old shapes of foul disease,
Ring out the narrowing lust of gold;
Ring out the thousand wars of old,
Ring in the thousand years of peace.

"In Memoriam"

Tennyson's passionate yearning for a new world without war derived from his deep Christian belief in a vanished order where war was unknown, a paradise lost in which lion had lain down with lamb and man nourished himself from the fruits of the earth. Most societies which memorialize their past seem to cherish a similar golden vision. In the culture of the west, the idea is most movingly conveyed in the idyllic poetry of the Greeks and in the pastorals of the Latin poets. Theocritus created a literary world in which nature provided "a framework for human emotions...amid pleasant and attractive scenery, suitable to provide an agreeable resting place for the weary. Among springs, gullies, mossy rocks and carpets of soft grass, shepherds lead a free and solitary life in the bosom of the valleys, knowing their animals by name, tending them and loving them." Virgil's *Georgics* celebrate a more organized but still sublime style of existence, "the annual round of labour in which the Italian yeoman's life was passed, bringing out the intimate relationship with nature into which man was brought in the course of that life and suggesting the delight to heart and imagination which he drew from it."

Forgotten for a thousand years, the Greek and Latin pastoralists inspired among Renaissance writers a new flowering of idyllic verse which centered on the idea of a lost Arcadia, whose inhabitants lived "innocent and voluptuous, with no hell or heaven" and no rumor of violence, let alone war, to disturb the absolutely even tenor of their days. In English literature, Milton's *Allegro* and *Penseroso* most exactly catch the Arcadian mood; in painting it is captured in its most exalted form by Poussin's perfection of composition and the endless, enchanted distances of Claude.

But a yearning for perpetual peace, past or yet to come, is not only artistic; it is also a central element of many of the world's great religions, as in the *Wu-Wei* (non-action) of Taoism and the insistence on *ahisma* (non-injury) common to Jainism and Buddhism. The great modern apostle of non-violence, Mahatma Gandhi, perceived the roots of his thinking in the Hindu *Bhagavad-Gita*, and particularly in the allegory of the battle between the Kauravas and the Pandavas which he believed preached the same message as Christ's

This tranquil vision of the Dutch countryside, with its idyllic elements of sheep, shepherds, waterfowl and windmills, encapsulates the national gratitude for peace, prosperity and independence that followed the Netherlands' eighty-year war against the Spanish. The ruined fortification in the foreground is perhaps a reminder that in 1573 Haarlem had sustained a seven-month siege by the Duke of Alva, who slaughtered the garrison when the city eventually fell.

Sermon on the Mount. That magnificent appeal to human self-abnegation was a major influence on his outlook, raised though he was in a non-Christian tradition. And Christ's own teaching embraced ideas which had also begun to appear in the public policy of the classical world, particularly in the peace proclamations of Ptolemaic Egypt (the *philanthropa*) and in the Roman concept of *pax*. The first, however, was an expression of benevolence by a stronger party to a weaker; the second depended upon legal agreement between consenting parties. Christian teaching was unique in that it rested on the idea of brotherhood and love, to be persisted in even when its object spurned the offering and reviled he who tendered it.

It has in consequence remained the most powerful source of all pacifist feelings, and also the most difficult to reconcile with public life, even that of believers. The early fathers of the Church, Tertullian foremost among them, denied indeed that violence might ever be justified or that a man might be both a Christian and a soldier. It was inevitable, in a state founded upon war, that a religion preaching such a doctrine would attract persecution. And, once Church and Empire had arrived at an accommodation in the fourth century, ways were found by theologians to blunt its rigor. St. Augustine of Hippo, the first great social theologian, was actually able to argue that war against the impious and infidel could be a just conflict. And in the thousand years of turmoil which followed the collapse of the Roman Empire, much of it the apparent work of heathen invaders, the concept of the holy war provided almost as much of a necessity as a convenience to the embattled Christian states which succeeded it.

The Church was always troubled, however, by the moral ambiguity of Christian fighting Christian, and gradually worked out, from the tenth century, a doctrine of the just war and the truce of God which did much to mitigate the medieval aristocracy's apparently insatiable lust for combat. The revival of humanism in the fifteenth century reinforced Christian teaching with Roman legal provisions for the restraint of violence. And the Renaissance mind was, as we have seen, also influenced to reject war as a natural and inevitable ingredient of human life by the rediscovery of idyll and pastoral. In Milton's *Ode on the Morning of Christ's Nativity*, the dual stream of Christian quietism and Arcadian Classicism sublimely combine:

But He, her fears to cease,
Sent down the meek-eyed Peace;
She, crown'd with olive green, came softly sliding
Down through the turning sphere,
Her ready harbinger,
With turtle wing the amorous clouds dividing;
And waving wide her myrtle wand,
She strikes a universal peace through sea and land.

For many of Milton's contemporaries, revulsion from war required more than a literary expression. Among the early Reformers, Calvin had taught passionately against war, though he was prepared to permit its waging for defensive purposes, a mitigation which his princely followers interpreted all too liberally. The exclusive sects of the seventeenth century, Mennonites, Anabaptists and particularly Quakers, returned to the teaching of the Sermon on the Mount in its exact literature. And, though they were made to suffer for their intransigence, their example awoke a belief in the possibility of peaceful co-existence between individuals and societies which underlies the work of all modern peace-seeking movements. Moreover, the comparatively peaceful condition of European states in the eighteenth century lent reality to their aspirations, after the horrors and chaos of the wars of religion in France and Germany. And mood and circumstances then combined to encourage a legal and political literature of diplomatic restraint. Crucé, a French monk of the seventeenth century, had proposed the abolition of war through the establishment of means for sovereigns to settle their differences by negotiation, an idea furthered by another Frenchman, Saint-Pierre, in his plan for a confederation of European states. As clergymen, both looked to religious sentiment to provide the motive force of their systems, even though the machinery was to be temporal. Immanuel Kant, the Prussian philosopher of the Enlightenment, advanced in his *Eternal Peace* (1795) a similar scheme of international federation, but founded on the imperatives of logic and reason.

Kant's work, and the similar arguments of Jeremy Bentham, generated a flowering of rationalist pacifist societies throughout Europe and America in the nineteenth century, dedicated to the settlement of international disputes by arbitration and to the achievement of general disarmament. And at the end of the century the measures agreed at the Hague Convention, amplifying the earlier provision of the Geneva Convention, did go some way toward achieving the latter aim. But by then a greater hope for peace had come to reside in the prevailing system of free trade, which was seen by its exponents as conferring benefits so visibly and tangibly preferable to the possible rewards of war as to render the latter unthinkable to all states belonging to the commercial world. The best known of the Free Trade pacifists, Norman Angell, actually argued in 1910 that the *de facto* internationalism of finance and commerce had made war impossible.

The vision of industry as an alternative outlet for man's harmful energies was, however, much older than Manchester School pacifism. The ant and the bee, and the harmonious cooperativeness of their economic life have long fascinated the human imagination and been held up as a mirror of society to mankind: "So work the honey-bees/Creatures that by a rule in nature teach/The act of order to a peopled Kingdom." (Shakespeare, *Henry V.*) The town, which could be seen as analagous to the hive, was commonly contrasted as a model of concord and security to the dangerous, factious country-side. And it was a fact undeniable to observers in the seventeenth or eighteenth centuries that the most peaceful and law-abiding states were also the most urbanized, notably Holland and England. That they were also aggressively imperialist was forgotten. It was the industriousness and prosperity of their domestic populations which impressed, and led the pioneers of economics to believe that the rise of industry would progressively lead men away from war. "If war enriched some of the peoples of antiquity," wrote Quesnay, founder of the French school of physiocrats whose work was to usher in the revolution they believed would utterly transform human society for the better, "it impoverishes and makes miserable the peoples of modern times." Comte, founder of the Positivist school and father of modern sociology, was even more adamant that the rise of industry was leading man away from war toward peace, through the enjoyment of the riches it produced. "In antiquity the greatest industrial efforts were related primarily to war, which gave rise to prodigious inventions, especially in connection with sieges. In modern times, on the contrary, the system of armaments is relatively less perfected than in Greek and Roman times, when we take into consideration the great industrial development."

Comte's anticipation of a broadening peacefulness based upon industrial enterprise and cooperation assumes retrospectively the appearance of benighted optimism. Had he looked more carefully he would have seen that the rise of industry in his own time had as its most notable product the great guns, land and shipborne, with which the kings of Europe had subdued their overmighty subjects and the explorers had won for them empires beyond the seas. Had he had but a little power to look ahead, he would have seen that the leaders of industry like Krupp and Armstrong were as ready to make a fortune in armaments as in ship or railway building, and that the scale of their earnings would inspire a new breed of inventors and manufacturers, like Nobel and Maxim, to choose the field of armaments from the outset in which to prospect for gold. Within fifty years of Comte's death in 1853, indeed, liberal opinion had already begun to look with suspicion on the captains of industry as positive instigators of conflict, seeking to enlarge artificially a market for their output by provoking wars when none arose in the natural course of things.

The Encyclopedists and Positivists had been misled in their analysis of the trend of industrialization by the appearance of harmonious cooperation it imposed upon human labor. Within the industrial system, individual antagonisms were seemingly averted by the division of labor and group competition by the automatic matching of demand to supply. What they had failed to foresee was that supply and demand might fall out of phase, and so provoke wants as intense as those which had underlain the old-fashioned wars of economic conquest they believed the world had put behind. What they failed to observe from the past and the present was that the discipline and comradeship of armies exemplified the principle of cooperation in its most perfected form, had always done so and would progressively come to represent the standard of comportment which factory owners desired to impose on their workers. Industry, in short, far from making men less military, increasingly made them more so during the nineteenth century. The mass armies of the twentieth century's world wars were to be its most impressive product.

Soldiers, and particularly the leaders of soldiers, would have disassociated themselves from this parallelism, for they have always chosen to emphasize the dash and bravado of military life, rather than the code of obedience and sanction which underlies it. And some forms of military organization do undoubtedly rest upon free will, or at least upon calculated self-interest, notably the militia system which furnished the armies of the Greek city-states, the Roman republic and the free Swiss cantons. But the city militiamen of antiquity were freed for war by their possession of household and agricultural slaves, and another form of bondage equally under-pinned the feudal military class of medieval Europe. In some societies, these roles were reversed. The great armies of the Turkish Ottoman empire were largely recruited from slaves, while conditions of service in the eighteenth century Russian army were little different from those of serfdom. It was indeed customary for Russian village priests to say the mass for the dead on the departure of youths nominated for military service, since the term was for life and their families were resigned by experience to abandon hope of seeing them again.

Western society, when it put warrior rule behind it at the end of the Middle Ages, chose to ignore for a time the apparently inevitable corollary of this shift — that if soldiers are not to be masters they must be made servants — by purchasing military skills on the open market. The mercenary system undoubtedly relieved the prosperous of direct military obligation while sparing the poorer from conscription. But its benefits proved illusory, as every employer of mercenaries discovered sooner rather than later. These bought soldiers' fickleness, usually but not necessarily financial, ultimately drove all states which sought real sovereignty to recognize that their armies must be made part of the political apparatus. Hence, during the seventeenth century, the appearance of what came to be called regular armies whose soldiers, though enlisted for pay, were maintained in permanent employment and subjected to legal and bureaucratic authority.

The ideal of peace may well have seemed fostered by this development, for the paid and disciplined soldier, housed apart from the rest of the population and supervised by officers who were functionaries of the state, offered much less of a threat to domestic tranquility than the rapacious freebooter into which the disgruntled mercenary all too easily turned when municipal or royal purses fell empty. The emergence of regular armies also appeared to reduce the incidence of foreign wars, they being too valuable to squander in specious quarrels, while they were undoubtedly superior to feudal or mercenary forces at protecting the frontiers of Christendom against barbaric and infidel intruders. But in the long run the regular system provided no better guarantee than any other of durable peace or freedom from widespread military obligation. For its trend proved to run inelectably toward the expansion of armies, as states vied against each other to maximize the institutions from which they derived security against their neighbors and control over the populations.

By the end of the nineteenth century, the regular armies of the great powers had in almost every case grown to a size which required the short-term enlistment of all fit youths in the population, who were recruited by compulsion and held liable to recall for duty in time of war almost into their middle age. Industry, which employed their labor in their years of maturity, had meanwhile become a source of military power secondary only to size of population; its output of cannon and armor-plate was everywhere exhibited as a proud symbol of national potency. Peace, as the world made its revolution into the twentieth century, seemed to have become the preoccupation only of ineffectual liberals and cranky optimists.

When I told the Captain that I thought myself engaged in the marines, "By Jasus, my lad," said he, "and you have had a narrow escape." He told me, that the regiment into which I had been so happy as to enlist was one of the oldest and boldest in the whole army, and that it was at that time serving in that fine, flourishing and plentiful country, Nova Scotia. He dwelt long on the beauties and riches of this terrestrial paradise, and dismissed me, perfectly enchanted with the prospect of a voyage thither.

William Cobbett on enlisting in the British Army in 1784.

Thomas Davies, *A View of the Hudson River.*

Limbourg brothers, *Harvest* from *Les Très Riches Heures du Duc de Berri*.

Davies, an officer in the Royal Artillery, was a member of the British garrison of North America during the Seven Years' War. This peaceful view of the Hudson [ABOVE] is probably of its lower reaches. Fort Ticonderoga, on its headwaters, of which Davies also painted a view, was the scene of heavy fighting in June and July, 1759, when Amherst captured it and Crown Point from the French. Topographical painting was a skill taught to both artillery and engineer officers as part of their professional training. The wealth of sketches they made in their off-duty hours provides many of our earliest views of remote places.

Books of Hours were popular medieval aids to devotion, which were often richly illuminated. The Book of Hours of the Duke of Berri (a famous contemporary patron of the arts) is the finest example of the genre, each page being devoted to activities characteristic of a season of the year. Here [ABOVE] the villeins of a rich landowner harvest his crops in the shadow of the walls of his castle. His power to protect their livelihood from marauding armies would remain the basis of the North European economy for another two hundred years.

Claude Gellée, *Aeneas at Delos*.

Domenichino, *Apollo and Neptune Building Troy*.

Legend held that Neptune and Apollo, upon whom Zeus had imposed a penalty of servitude to men for causing the death of his sons, agreed with King Laomedon of Troy to build the walls of the city [OPPOSITE]. The king later withheld the fee he had promised the gods and Neptune sided with the Greeks against the Trojans in the subsequent war.

The supreme master of the pastoral subject and mood in European art, Claude here treats a famous poetic theme from antiquity [ABOVE]. After escaping from the besieged city of Troy, Aeneas reached Delos, where he, his father Anchises and son Ascanius were shown the Temple of Apollo. The oracle of the god there instructed him to begin his pilgrimage in search of the mother of the Trojan race, which forms the story of Virgil's *Aeneid*.

Lloyd George informed us that he had consulted the Governor and the Deputy-Governor of the Bank of England, as well as other outstanding personalities of the City known for their experience, and also the most qualified representatives of the cotton, steel, coal, etc., industries in northern England, Glasgow, etc. They were all *horrified* by the prospects of our participation in the European conflict. Such participation, they told him, would shatter the country's financial structure, whose centre lies in London. It would ruin our commerce and industries, deal a blow to labour, salaries and prices, and would inevitably lead to trouble and violence by wintertime....

Lord Morley on a British Cabinet Meeting, July 28, 1914.

Hieronymus Bosch, *The Garden of Delights* (left panel).

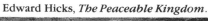

Edward Hicks, *The Peaceable Kingdom*.

This triptych panel, conceived and executed in a style of high fantasy [OPPOSITE], depicts the state of man before the Fall, inhabiting a fruitful garden among beasts and birds living in perfect harmony with each other.

Hicks, the master painter of the naive, was a Pennsylvanian who started life as a coach-sign and ornamental painter, then combined that trade with painting historical and religious subjects. Nineteenth-century America was fertile ground for realistic and particularly pacifist sects, and Hicks became a devout Quaker during the course of his life — appropriately enough, because his state was a seventeenth-century Quaker foundation.

His vision of wild animals and humans fraternizing [ABOVE] symbolizes the spirit of the relationship William Penn established with the native Indians at the time of settlement.

Denis Diderot was the most dynamic and productive of the French rationalists of the eighteenth century, and his supreme achievement was the *Encyclopedia*, in which were collected the most advanced ideas and up-to-date information of the age. Its informing theme was that of progress toward a world of political and social justice, from which war and tyranny would be banished. The Encyclopedists believed that an important means to their end was the dissemination of the most recent and exact technical knowledge, which would allow the harnessing of human energies to peaceful and profitable activity. These engravings, notable for their own remarkable technical quality, depict a heavy smithy [RIGHT], where hubs are being bored, rims forged and wheels shod, a bakery [BELOW], and the practice of bee-keeping [OPPOSITE ABOVE].

French illustrations from Diderot's "Encyclopedia."

This engraving of a sixteenth-century Italian cannon foundry [RIGHT] shows all the more important types of artillery of the period and several of the manufacturing processes. On the left is a large siege mortar, in the center a battering cannon, on the right three culverins. The wheel on the left, worked by a boy, supplies power, probably for the forced draft of the forge in the background. In the right background the products of the foundry are seen at work; the style of fortification is an early modification of traditional forms to the artillery age.

Giovanni Stradanano, *Cannon Foundry*.

Enameled bricks, Persian archers.

We at Concord heard they was a-coming. The Bell rung at 3 o'clock for an alarm. As I was then a Minuteman, I was soon in town and found my captain and the rest of my company at the post. It wasn't long before there was other minute companies. One company, I believe, of minute men was raised in almost every town to stand at a minute's warning. Before sunrise there was, I believe, 150 of us and more of all that was there.

We thought we would go and meet the British. We marched down towards Lexington about a mile and a half, and we see them a-coming. We halted and stayed there until we got within about 100 rods, then we was ordered to the about face and marched before them with our drums and fifes a-going and also the British. We had grand music.

Amos Barrett, at Concord, April 19, 1775.

Darius I's Persian reign followed social and artistic traditions established by the Assyrian Empire in the seventh and eighth centuries B.C., the most militaristic society the world had ever seen. Darius' armies conquered the Indus Valley, and he attempted to conquer Greece but lost his fleet in a storm, and his army was defeated at Marathon in 1490 B.C.

Nubia lay beyond Egypt's military frontier on the upper Nile, but was coveted by the Pharoahs because of its gold mines. This battle scene [RIGHT] is stylized; the Egyptians fought in formed ranks.

These works [BELOW] of the Old Stone Age, which date from at least the tenth century B.C., were discovered in a cave near Santander, Spain, in 1879. Their exact purpose is disputed, but there is general agreement that it was magical and religious, designed to give success in the chase to the hunter, who appears in some of the paintings with arrows or spear, the earliest representation we have of man as a wielder of weapons.

Painted casket from the tomb of Tutankhamen, battle between Egyptians and Nubians.

Altamira cave painting, bison.

Greek vase.

Black-figure paintings of heavily armed Athenian hoplites of the sixth century in combat [LEFT]. The round, broad sword and thrusting spear were standard equipment. The infantrymen, who fought in dense ranks, also wore breastplates and leg greaves.

The swimmers [BELOW] presumably belong to siege engineering corps of the Assyrian army. They are swimming under the surface of the moat protecting an enemy castle, perhaps to begin work on undermining the walls. The lower figure is breathing from an inflated animal skin.

Assyrian low relief sculptural decoration, underwater swimmers (detail).

Greek vase (detail).

The detail from the Greek vase [ABOVE] illustrates the companions of Hercules in combat with the Amazons.

Italian tournament
(detail).

When I recall the day on which we saw the troops march away from here in their glittering uniforms and all the freshness of youth, each man filled with hopes of winning fame and honour, and now! We stared at the poor wretches, their heads and feet wrapped in tatters, the upper part of the body covered with rags of every possible material or else with straw matting. Even hides, still full of dried blood, covered their nakedness. The expression in their pallid features was a terrible one, their eyes stared from their white, lined faces as if they could still see all the horrors which had lain in wait for them on the icy steppes of Russia; and their words sounded hollow and rough, as though cries of pain had made them hoarse.

Louis von Kaisenberg, on the return of Napoleon's Grand Army from Moscow, Kassel, February 18, 1813.

English book frontispiece, *The Eglinton Tournament*.

Chinese silk scroll painting, *Wrestling Before the Emperor* (detail).

A mock combat between knights was first recorded in Wurzburg in 1127. It quickly achieved universal popularity among the European noble class; the joust, a combat between two knights, appeared as a feature of tournaments only in the fourteenth century. But both forms served the purpose of entertaining a society whose chief interest was war. This decorated chest [OPPOSITE ABOVE] shows an Italian tournament at the moment of the *mêlée*.

In 1839, inspired by the contemporary resurgence of interest in medieval chivalry, the 13th Earl of Eglinton staged a tournament at his castle in Ayrshire, Scotland [OPPOSITE BELOW]. Guests impersonated famous knights of the past, who jousted for the favor of a "Queen of Beauty." Intended as high romance, the proceedings ended in farce.

Wrestlers grapple for the entertainment of a Manchu emperor [ABOVE]; the entertainment also included archery.

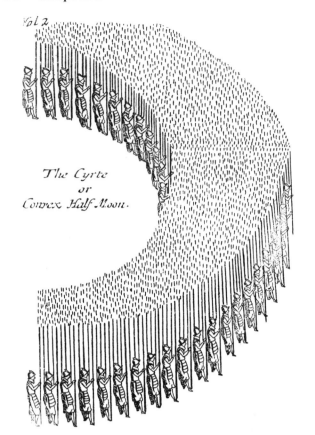

The Convex Half Moon.

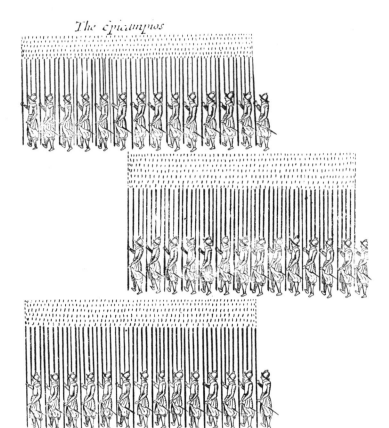

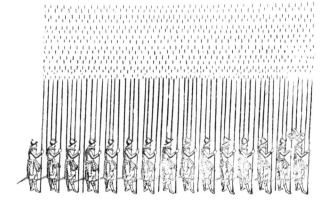

Vol 2

The Battail call'd Plinthium

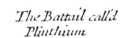

The Battle Called Plintium.

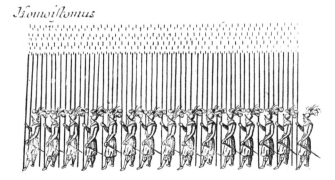

English manuscript engravings from John Potter's "Antiquities of Greece."

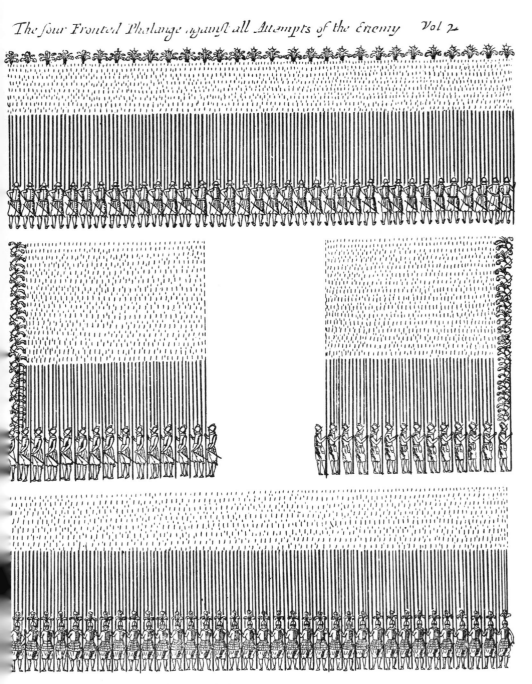

The four Fronted Phalange against all Attempts of the Enemy   Vol 2

The Four-fronted Phalange.

Interest in the military practice of antiquity was stimulated by the revival of classical learning. It was believed that the study of Greek and Roman warfare would yield secrets applicable to the current age. The engraver has dressed his hoplites as pikemen of the English Civil War. The book from which these engravings came was written by a classical scholar who was Archbishop of Canterbury and who had a special interest in military strategy.

Louis Le Nain, *The Forge*.

Japanese screen painting, armorers at work
(detail).

Louis Le Nain, one of the three artist
brothers, depicted scenes of French peasant
life with a beautiful and sympathetic realism.
This interior of a village forge [OPPOSITE] is
inspired by the idea of the dignity of peaceful
labor.

A Japanese screen painting showing artisans manufacturing the components of
samurai armor [LEFT], followed by another
[BELOW] representing the forging and grinding of
swords. Each Japanese sword was regarded
as having a personality and was given its own
name. These works are part of a series
depicting artisans.

Japanese screen painting, swordsmiths (detail).

Italian manuscript illumination, foundry (detail).

An early cannon foundry [LEFT]. Bronze is being smelted in the block furnace fed by faggots. Cannon balls and a large-calibre, two-part bombard represent the product of the foundry's moulds.

Famous for his mystical pictures set in the scenery and peopled by the villagers of the Thames Valley, Spencer also worked with war themes. From his First World War experience he created the resurrection sequence of the Burghclere Chapel (see page 212). During the Second World War he produced a series of paintings of shipbuilding on the

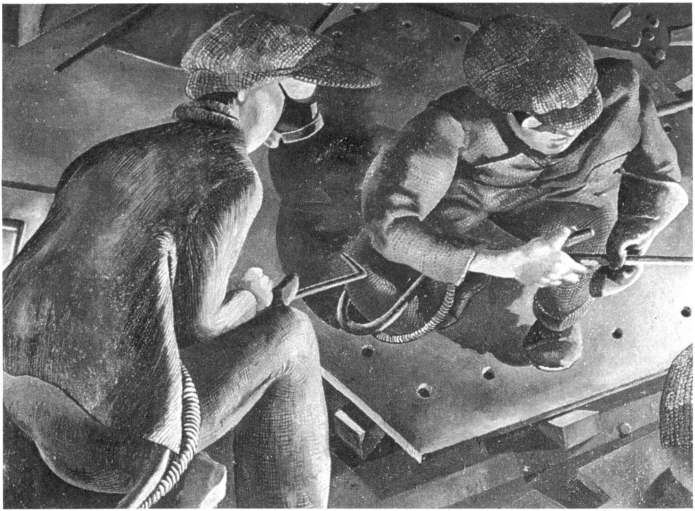

Stanley Spencer, *The Burners* from *Shipbuilding on the Clyde* (left panel).

Clyde, of which this is the left panel of the
first triptych [OPPOSITE BELOW]. It conveys the
urgency with which Britain's shipworkers
toiled to replace the losses caused by the
German U-Boat campaign.

Alfred Krupp inherited a bankrupt firm
employing six workers in Essen in 1826 and
turned it into one of the greatest engineering
businesses in the world, largely by his success in manufacturing armaments for the
bellicose Kingdom of Prussia. This
nineteenth-century woodcut [BELOW] shows
the house from which the enterprise grew,
surrounded by trucks of shell castings.

Mann, *The Original Krupp House*.

John Collett, *The Press Gang*.

In time of emergency the Royal Navy was empowered to "press" members of the seafaring population into its ranks. Collet's Hogarthian scene in a waterside inn [ABOVE] shows two seamen, in their distinctive loose breeches, bringing a captive before their officer, while another begs for the "pressed" man's release.

Traditionally and, in many armies, legally, military musicians were not soldiers, even though uniformed. It was therefore common to enlist boys below military age as drummers and fifers. Manet's fifer [OPPOSITE] wears the blue dress uniform and *bonnet de police* of Napoleon III's army just before its destruction in the Franco-Prussian War.

Edouard Manet, *The Fifer*.

Rembrandt van Rijn, *Jacob and Esau*.

The figure of Esau [ABOVE] is in hunting costume, and the bow he carries had already gone out of date in Rembrandt's time as a weapon of war. The interest that Rembrandt had in figures of warriors in antiquity and modern times is evident in this drawing of a biblical subject.

Gillray, son of a soldier who had fought at Fontenoy, was a satirical and political engraver of prodigious output. Here [OPPOSITE ABOVE] his target is the home defense force hastily decreed into existence – at least on paper – at the beginning of the French invasion scare during the Revolutionary War. A cobbler, plasterer, tailor and barber march in the front rank, flanking Hoppner, a Royal Academician.

Eighteenth-century armies were enlisted, at least in theory, by voluntary recruitment [OPPOSITE BELOW]. Drink and an advance of pay were the inducements.

James Gillray, *Supplementary Militia*.

Johannes Elias Ridinger, *Recruiting*.

Upon the 25th day of March, 1694, and came to the Regiment then Quartered in the Cannongate Edenburgh the day following, and the next day was Shewn to Sir James with severall other Recruits.

Upon Sir James's takeing a view of me, he was pleased to Say to Ensigne Haliday, "What my friend Haliday, do you bring me Children for Soldiers? I did not Expect this from You, for You know Wee want men," Ensigne Haliday answered in an Humble Manner, that he must Confess I was too Young, but that it was Interely my own Desire and that my Parents could not diswade me from it, therefore they Desirous I should be under His Honour's Care, whereupon Sir James asked Whose Childe I was and if he had any knowledge of my parents, the Ensigne told Sir James my father's name, whom Sir James knew, and said he knew my Grandfather also, whereupon Sir James turned to me with a frown, and Said, "You young Rogue, how came you to Run away from your Parents?" I answered him I did not run away, but came with their Consent to be a Soldier. "A Soldier!" says Sir James with a Smileing Contenance, "go home, Young rogue, and go to School."

Sergeant John Wilson, on joining the 15th Foot.

Frans Hals, *The Company of St. Joris*.

The right to raise a militia for the defense of a city was one of the most cherished of concessions in the Middle Ages, since it established a degree of citizen independence. By the seventeenth century, when Hals painted these rich burghers of Haarlem mustered for parade [LEFT], the militias were already declining into ceremonial bodies, their role overtaken by the regular and mercenary armies of the state.

The celebrated naive painter, Rousseau, here splendidly captures the restored efficiency and morale of the French army after the defeat of 1870 [BELOW]. The "third gun of the fourth battery" of the regiment is about to be replaced by the revolutionary 75mm; the conscripts are fit and alert; the N.C.O. on the left wears the medals of a colonial campaign. Rousseau himself had served in the Mexican expedition, 1861-7, as a regimental bandsman, and as a sergeant in the defense of France, 1870-1.

Henri Rousseau, *Artillerymen*.

Etching, *The Allied Sovereigns at Paris*.

German wood engraving, *Austro-Prussian Peace Conference*.

Unknown, *The Field of the Cloth of Gold*.

After Napoleon's second expulsion from France in 1815, the kings of the states allied against him met to agree on an alliance system that would preserve the peace of Europe against demagogues. Here [OPPOSITE ABOVE] the King of Prussia and the Emperors of Austria and Russia admonish the twice-restored Louis XVIII.

In 1866 Prussia provoked war with Austria as a means of excluding her from German affairs. A single battle at Königgrätz, July 3, procured the desired result. Moltke, the victor, and Bismarck, the engineer of the crisis, here dictate terms to the Austrian representatives [OPPOSITE BELOW].

This meeting [ABOVE] between Henry VIII of England and Francis I of France at Calais, June 7, 1520, was typical of diplomatic encounters in the days of absolute monarchy. Though intended as a means toward an alliance, which it achieved, the meeting was largely a competition in display.

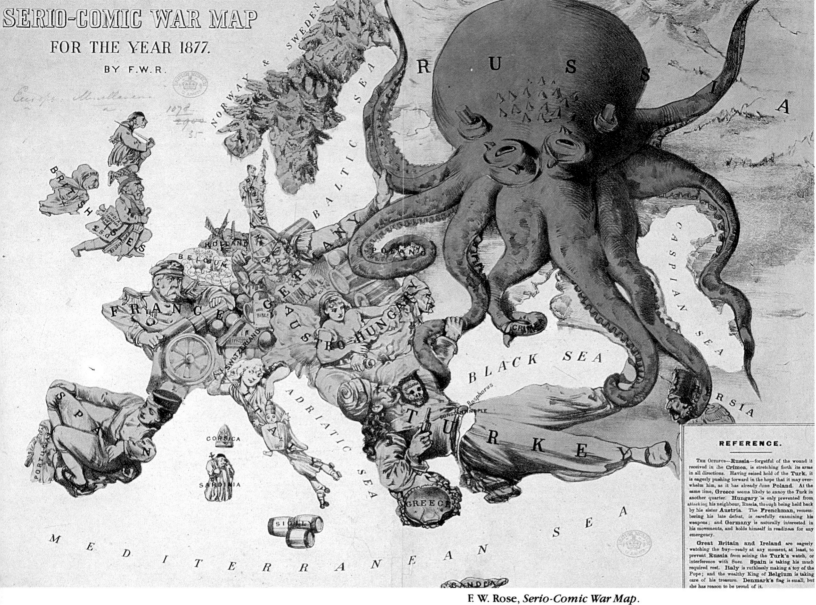

F. W. Rose, *Serio-Comic War Map*.

I saw people running along the Rue Vivienne; I promptly ran after them. The steps of the Stock Exchange, from top to bottom, were a sea of bare heads, with hats flung into the air and every voice raised in a tremendous *Marseillaise*, the roar of which drowned the buzz of noise from the stockbrokers' enclosure inside the building. I have never seen such an outburst of enthusiasm. One kept running into men pale with emotion, children hopping around in excitement and women making drunken gestures. Capoul was singing the *Marseillaise* from the top of an omnibus in the Place de la Bourse; on the Boulevard, Marie Sasse was singing it standing in her carriage, practically carried along by the delirium of the mob.

Edmond de Goncourt on the outbreak of the Franco-Prussian War, Paris, August 6, 1870.

Honoré Daumier, *The New Aerodynamics*.

Norman Lindsay, untitled.

Eighteen seventy-seven was a year of war in Europe. The Russians fought the Turks in the Balkans, and in the following year the European powers, in congress at Berlin, adjudicated a settlement. Its main purpose was to limit the growing power of Russia, represented in the map [OPPOSITE ABOVE].

Daumier, the most famous and powerful of nineteenth-century cartoonists, represents the peace of Europe balanced on the point of a bayonet [OPPOSITE BELOW].

Lindsay, a member of a celebrated Australian family of artists, produced a series of anti-German posters during the First World War, designed to attract recruits to the Australian army [LEFT].

POLITICAL-DREAMINGS! _VISIONS OF

! PERSPECTIVE HORRORS !

The withdrawal of Austria and Russia from war with Napoleon during 1801 left Britain alone in the field. Gillray here represents what may well have been Pitt's state of mind as he steeled himself for the negotiations that resulted in the Peace of Amiens in the following year.

James Gillray, *Political Dreams*.

II
Outbreak

William Hogarth, *March of the Guards to Finchley.*

I have always heard it said," wrote Luigi da Porto, an Italian historian of the sixteenth century, "that peace brings riches; riches brings pride; pride brings anger; anger brings war; war brings poverty; poverty brings humanity; humanity brings peace; peace, as I have said, brings riches, and so the world's affairs go round." His analysis has a persuasive if cynical symmetry. But he was writing of his own time and region, already a place of sophisticated statecraft, diplomacy and legally regulated relationships between one power and another. "Peace" and "war" were, to its inhabitants, each a clearly defined and highly distinct set of circumstances, and passage from one to the other a process to be undergone only with deliberation and due ceremony.

Writing a century later, in a time of trouble over much of Northern Europe, Hobbes proposed a different explanation of war's causality. Far from seeing war as an interruption of peace, he viewed it as man's natural state from which he was released only when he agreed to surrender his liberty to fight his neighbor — in the interests of self-preservation — to a power stronger than both of them, the Leviathan, or sovereign, from which his book took its title. Poverty, in his scheme of things, was indeed the result of war, but of a war of all against all which stifled humanity and so, far from bringing peace, interminably sustained the "fear and danger of violent death" with which mankind in the primitive state was condemned to live. Of course, the primal world of the *Leviathan* was an artificial construction of Hobbes' imagination, and perhaps no condition of human existence has ever quite matched its awfulness; family and tribal feeling everywhere mitigate the dreadful isolation of Hobbes' natural man. But what anthropologists tell us of inter-tribal relations in the primitive world confirms that Hobbes was nearer the truth than da Porto. For to them "peace" and "war" are not separate and distinct, but elements in a social continuum of which "force and fraud," Hobbes' two cardinal military virtues, are the defining constants.

We can therefore scarcely speak of the "outbreak" of war until, by paradox, we approach the beginning of what we call the civilized

Hogarth's highly characteristic genre scene shows the Foot Guards, recalled hastily from service against the French in the Low Countries, leaving London to meet the army of the Young Pretender ("Bonnie Prince Charlie") marching south from Scotland. The incidents depicted are exaggerated but perhaps not much so; contemporary military movements were always encumbered by civilians, womenfolk seeking to accompany their men, and sutlers who lived by the sale of goods to the soldiers. The military figures in the foreground are a fifer and boy drummer, in the heavily laced coats of musicians; a soldier of the grenadier company in his distinctive miter hat; an officer armed with a half-pike as a symbol of his rank; and another, worse for wear, attended by his soldier-servant.

age. And then, even among the Greeks and Romans, we find war regarded as the prevailing climate of politics, and peace as no more than a temporary alleviation of its rigors. The common experience of antiquity explains this attitude. During the century and a half between the last Persian war (480-479 B.C.) and the battle of Chaeronea (338 B.C.), Athens was at war on the average of two years out of every three, and enjoyed no period of peace longer than ten years. During the whole of Roman history until the foundation of the Empire in the first century A.D., the Temple of Janus, whose opening "signified that Rome had taken up arms" and its closure that "peace reigned all about her," was shut on only two occasions, once after the wars with Carthage and once after the battle of Actium.

The Greeks, moreover, were resigned to the parallel phenomenon of "private" war and to its often greater prevalence over "public" war. Brigandage and piracy were not even regarded by them as particularly dishonorable, so that "from Cilicia to Caria in the Black Sea, in the islands of the Aegean and particularly around Crete, from Aetiolia to the Valley of the Po, from the mouth of the Tiber to the Delta of the Rhone, in Corsica, in Sardinia and in the Lipari islands, not to mention the African coast, men held themselves ready to raid, more or less as if that were their craft." (Livy.) These were exactly the areas over most of which, two thousand years later, Moslem and Christian pirates would ply their trade against each other's merchantmen, and for the same reason that the descendants of Odysseus had felt free to do so: the absence from the Mediterranean of an imperial power strong enough to maintain naval control across the whole length of the inland sea. Rome established such a navy, and an army which drove brigandage into the remotest mountain corners of her empire. On her collapse, order broke down throughout the once civilized world and "private" war became once again an endemic ingredient of European life until the establishment of modern states in the seventeenth century. Even then, after the new monarchies had broken the power of local potentates to fight each other when they chose, piracy continued to flourish in the Mediterranean until the beginning of the nineteenth century, while organized banditry persisted in places until the establishment of regular police forces.

The motives of private war require no exposition; loot and adventure comprehend them almost entirely. Public war has deeper and more complex origins. Among primitive peoples, without lands to protect or envy for those of neighbors, war was — and in some remote parts still is — an ingredient of everyday life, taking the form of sporadic raiding and ambush, and occasionally of ritual confrontation between tribal warriors at pre-arranged rendez-vous. Population pressures transformed this activity into something far more destructive, which the settled lands of Europe and China experienced in the millennia before and after the birth of Christ as massive barbarian eruptions, successfully resisted in the east but to which the Roman empire ultimately succumbed. The kingdoms which succeeded it remained for centuries on a warrior footing, harassed by intruders from the steppe, the desert and the northern seas, and needing little pretext to fight each other over issues of lordship and territorial infringement.

Religion was the first immaterial force to elevate the pretext for war to a higher plane. Inevitably intermingled with territorial drives, it had nonetheless overlain at a conscious level the great Arab conquests of the Middle East and Mediterranean lands in the seventh and eighth centuries A.D. And with the political stabilization of France, Italy and Northern Europe after 1000 A.D., it provided the impetus for the Christian counter-attack against Islam which we call the Crusades. Originally initiated to reclaim the Holy Land and its sacred places for Christendom, Crusade subsequently came to mean any war against infidels or heretics to which papal authority gave sanction. The expansion of the German kingdoms into Central Europe and the reconquest of Spain from the Moors thus came to enjoy ecclesiastical endorsement. And when, in the fifteenth and sixteenth centuries, the Portuguese and Spaniards took ship across the oceans to plant the flag of empire in north and south America, in India and China, they also claimed to do so as the standard-bearers of true religion.

Their great imperial adventure coincided, however, with the outbreak in Europe of bitter dissent over what constituted true religion, which would fuel the urge to conflict between Catholics and Protestants for the next two hundred years. It coincided as well with the emergence of the new centralist states, transformed militarily by their establishment of standing armies but also juridically by their institution of elaborate legal codes and the apparatus of diplomacy. The later Middle Ages had seen the beginnings of formal diplomatic exchange administered by legates of the papacy or the supranational bodies of heralds. The general acceptance by reigning monarchs of ambassadors from neighboring courts both inaugurated and reflected a new international understanding. The Greeks and Romans had, of course, practiced diplomacy. But its basis was distorted in the Roman world by the Empire's refusal to regard an alliance as anything but a means of subjecting the other contracting party to satellite status. And while it was the Greeks who largely invented the terminology of modern diplomatic usage, their insatiable appetite for trickery and double-dealing in the pursuit of short-term advantage worked absolutely contrary to the spirit of conciliation and settlement which should properly inform it. "The average Greek's loyalty to his own city," wrote the British diplomatist, Sir Harold Nicolson, "was so intense, that he regarded all other Hellenes as potential enemies and all barbarians as natural slaves." Such attitudes were not uncharacteristic of the Italian city-states of the early Renaissance, to whose governors Machiavelli preached a doctrine of statecraft which Demosthenes would have applauded. By the end of the seventeenth century, however, the European kingdoms had moved beyond calculations of narrow and selfish expediency to accept that, whatever their differences over religious belief and however antagonistic their strategic and commercial aims, all shared an interest in the maintenance of peace. Conversely all recognized that war, with its risks, expense and legacy of rancor, was an enterprise to be undertaken only after the exhaustion of every other means of persuasion, and even then with gravity and due ceremony.

Hence the appearance of warfare in its classic European form, typified by the "succession" wars of the eighteenth century and the "cabinet" wars of the nineteenth. Waged by long-service, tightly disciplined, beautifully uniformed regular armies, their outbreak was the culmination of elaborate diplomatic ritual, in which resident ambassadors presented the sovereigns to whom they were accredited with elaborate expressions of their own royal masters' pained displeasure, took their leave when negotiations broke down with exchanges of mutual courtesy and were then escorted across the frontier with courtly decorum. Long gone were the days when ambassadors were selected from the commercial or even servant class, a type exemplified at its worst by Dr. de Puebla, the "filthy and unkempt" representative of Spain at the court of Henry VII of England who, on the ambassador's departure, voiced the hope that his successor might be a man "more fitted for human society." In the eighteenth century they were drawn from the hereditary nobility, and by the nineteenth they had come to form almost a hereditary class of their own, intimately acquainted with each other, speaking a common language and steeped in a delicate protocol of concession and diplomatic rupture.

By the nineteenth century, their military counterparts had also come strangely to resemble each other. The international and mercenary generals who had played so large a part in warfare until the end of the seventeenth century had disappeared to be replaced by a domestic breed of salaried and strictly trained professionals, with rigid expectations of how operations should proceed from the moment hostilities were declared. First came the proclamation of mobilization (though that itself might be invoked as an earnest of intent before diplomatic measures were exhausted). While the reservists thus summoned were gathered in, the standing army would concentrate in "covering positions" on the national frontier and its patrols perhaps skirmish with the enemy's on the other side. When the field army was mustered at full strength, the reservists broken in to marching and rehearsed in their drills and the depots stocked with supplies, the commander and his staff would deploy their forces for action, either attack or defense as circumstances dictated, and battle would ensue after the clash of advance guards.

Railway building much accelerated the initiation of hostilities as the century drew on, while the extension of the telegraph system allowed the commanders to spread their troops more widely over a front than ever before, besides offering politicians a chance to intervene directly in the conduct of operations; during the American Civil War Abraham Lincoln was at times in daily touch with four separate armies. But modern technology did not appear to contemporaries to threaten any drastic change to the essential function of war as they perceived it, which was to procure the settlement of disputes not resolvable by peaceful means. Thus in 1914 all the procedures hallowed by two hundred years of structured international intercourse – the exchange of notes, issue of ultimata, institution of "state of siege" and proclamation of general mobilization – were meticulously carried through in the evident belief that the war to which they were a prelude would be short, decisive and of bearable cost.

The First World War was violently to discredit that belief, and with it the system of "secret diplomacy" which the post-war leaders of the democracies alleged had brought it about. "Open covenants openly arrived at," President Wilson's challenging demand for a new spirit in international affairs, gave impetus to the creation of a League of Nations, whose mobilization of international public opinion would, it was hoped, make aggressive war impossible in the future. But the onward march of technology, acting together with the bitter rancors left by the war, meanwhile served to encourage the defeated and disappointed parties to the "unequal" peace of 1919 to think of using revolutionary weapons as a means of recovering lost or foregone advantages, and of maximizing their effect by opening hostilities without formal declaration of war. Surprise attack is as old as the hills, or at least as man's hunting ancestors who inhabited them. Its reappearance in the warfare of civilized states was not therefore revolutionary, as the propagandists of the totalitarian states alleged, but a retrograde step. And it was not even to prove, in the long run, of benefit to those who took it, for the outrage it provoked ensured an intensity of response and intolerance toward the defeated far more painful than the diplomatic inequity they had used to justify its adoption.

The abrogation of the old formality had a wider and more enduring effect. Colonial and imperial warfare had never exhibited its niceties, any more than had popular uprising, revolution or civil war. It was indeed the lack of warning, visible leadership and clear focus of resistance which made revolt so disliked by regular soldiers when called upon to suppress it, just as it was their colonial enemies' readiness to break all rules of diplomatic and military practice, as understood by Europeans, which convinced empire-building generals of the inherent untrustworthiness of their Asian and African adversaries. That empire-building was, to its victims, a straightforward act of conquest was a point of view with which few European politicians and soldiers had sympathized during the great age of expansion. All the more galling was it therefore when, in what has come to be called the age of decolonization, subject peoples all over the globe began to adopt the methods of revolution, as well as the weapons of modern technology, to wage wars of national liberation against their European overlords. None, needless to say, was begun with a formal declaration or carried on in a style which permitted its familiar pattern of mobilization, concentration and deployment to take its customary effect. As taught or practiced by the great guerrilla leaders of the Far East, Mao Tse-tung and Vo Nguyen Giap, the warfare of national liberation was designed to nullify large-scale manoeuvre and the superiority of numbers and equipment which underlay it. Chasing will-o'-the-wisps through paddy fields and rain forest, European soldiers were quickly reduced to a despair of frustration, beside which the certainties of traditional warfare, whatever their cost in blood, came to seem temptingly preferable.

But even in the theaters where regular armies were concentrated after 1945 and "conventional" operations therefore likely, it no longer seemed the case that commanders or their subordinates could expect decent warning of the outbreak of hostilities. Surprise attack marked the opening of the four Arab-Israeli wars of 1948-73, by which the general peace of the world was most seriously threatened, and in the aftermath of the last, it became the common expectation that a wider war would have the same inception. It is difficult to hope that the ethics of Pearl Harbor and Operation Barbarossa have been put aside when the world's two greatest powers maintain on hair-trigger alert armories of missiles, the release of which would bring about the almost total destruction of their populations within half an hour of a decision to launch.

Francisco Goya, *The Second of May.*

Napoleon's occupation of Spain in March, 1808 provoked fierce popular resentment, which erupted in widespread violence against the French garrison of Madrid on May 2-3. Goya was an eye-witness, and this scene [ABOVE] shows citizens attacking a party of French cavalry, Mamelukes of the Imperial Guard, in the foreground, and a *Chasseur à Cheval* (Dragoon), top right. That night and the following day the French garrison repaid their losses, which totaled a hundred and fifty, by mass executions.

Defeat in the Russo-Japanese War of 1904-5 precipitated discontents that had been festering for many years inside the Tsarist empire. Widespread industrial demonstrations and strikes culminated in the abortive revolution, put down by the army with extreme severity in some places. Soviet art has idealized the episode [OPPOSITE ABOVE] representing it as a prodrome of the Bolshevik revolution of 1917.

This polemical print [OPPOSITE BELOW] shows the attack by the Manchester and Cheshire

G.A. Knyazhevsky, F.M. Kulagin and V.N. Gorov, *Weavers' Strike, 1905* (detail).

George Cruikshank, *Peterloo Massacre*.

Yeomanry Cavalry on a parliamentary reform meeting at St. Peter's Field, Manchester, August 16, 1819. Eleven people were killed and five hundred injured after the Yeomanry and a regiment of regular cavalry were ordered by the magistrates to charge the crowd. The outrage has become known as the Peterloo Massacre.

Matthew Paris, *The Capture of the Cross by Saladin*.

I, with my detachment and ten Pensioners, was posted in the courtyard of the Bastille facing the door. I had behind me three guns firing two-pound balls. These were to be served by a dozen of my soldiers to prevent the beseigers rushing in, should they break down the gates. In order to checkmate the plan which the besiegers seemed to wish to carry out, after the second attack I caused two holes to be made in the raised drawbridge through which I intended to point my guns. However, being unable to get near enough owing to the tilting of the bridge, I replaced the guns by two siege guns loaded with grapeshot. We could not make much use of them, because only a few of the besiegers showed themselves. Moreover they had brought up a cart full of burning straw, with which they had set the Governor's house on fire, and placed it directly in front of the drawbridge, thus preventing us from seeing them. They had also brought up three cannon firing eight-pounder balls and a mortar, which they had posted in the garden of the Arsenal. Towards evening they fired a few rounds from this weapon, but did no damage. The fort replied with a few rounds of cannon fire. The besiegers seeing that their own artillery was ineffective, reverted to their original plan of storming the gates.

Louis de Flue,
Swiss Officer of the Bastille garrison,
July 14, 1789.

The Crusaders' capture of Jerusalem and establishment of the Latin Kingdom sparked the unification of the Moslems of Syria and Egypt who, under the leadership of Saladin, mounted a major counter-offensive against the Christian colonists at the end of the twelfth century. Saladin's victory at Hattin, July 4, 1187 [ABOVE LEFT], inflicted a setback on the Crusading movement from which it never fully recovered.

E. Krell after Francois Dubois of Amiens, *The Massacre of St. Bartholomew's Eve*.

On August 23-4, 1572 the royal army attacked the members of the Protestant party in Paris and slaughtered its leaders and thousands of their followers [LEFT]. Though the atrocity heightened the divisions between Catholic and Protestant in France, it also gave the Protestant leadership to Henry of Navarre, who would eventually reconcile the two. The massacre nevertheless provided the Protestant movement in Europe with some of its most powerful demonological images, of which this is an example.

The last and most important obstacle on the march of the First Crusade to Jerusalem was the city of Antioch. It withstood an eight-month siege, from October, 1097 to June, 1098 [BELOW], until surrendered by treachery.

French manuscript illumination, *The Siege and Capture of Antioch*.

Lieutenant Cholat, *The Storming of the Bastille*.

French etching, *The Execution of Louis XIV*.

A contemporary eye-witness view by an amateur painter of the attack on and capture of the royal fortress of the Bastille, Paris, by the revolutionary crowd, July 14, 1789 [OPPOSITE]. The fortress, which held only forty prisoners and was garrisoned by a handful of pensioners and Swiss Guards, was overcome by a well-armed mob that included many soldiers of the *Gardes Française*. Its fall is regarded as marking the outbreak of the French Revolution.

The radicalization of the French Revolution culminated in the trial of the king and his execution on January 21, 1793 [ABOVE]. The infantry and cavalry wear the uniforms of the old royal army, differentiated by the revolutionary cockade.

Unknown, *Incident in the Boxer Rebellion*.

George Scott, *Butler's Final Crossing of the Tugel*.

In 1900 the Boxers, a populist Chinese anti-foreign movement enjoying clandestine official support, laid siege to the European embassies in Peking. An international relief expedition was organized and entered Peking on August 28. It had been opposed ineffectually on the way at Yang T'sun, August 5, an episode here idealized [OPPOSITE ABOVE] by an official Social Realist painter of the Communist regime. Japanese, German and French soldiers and sailors are yielding to the Boxer attack.

A battery of British horse artillery is crossing a pontoon bridge under Boer fire [OPPOSITE BELOW]. Though a highly dramatized representation, the picture is documentary, and the details are depicted with an accuracy characteristic of the military art of the period. The drivers of the leading team are wearing the khaki service dress first generally issued for the campaign.

John Trumbull, *The Battle of Bunker's Hill* (detail).

The provincials in the redoubt and the lines reserved their fire till the enemy had come within about ten or twelve yards and then discharged them at once upon them. The fire threw their body into very great confusion, and all of them after having kept a fire for some time retreated in very great disorder down to the point where they landed, and some of them even got into their boats.

At this time their officers were observed by spectators on the opposite shore to come down and then to use the most passionate gestures, and even to push forward the men with their swords.

At length, by their exertions, the troops were again rallied and marched up to the entrenchments. The Americans reserved their fire and a second time put the regulars to flight, who once more retreated in precipitation to the boats.

Peter Thacher, eye-witness of Bunker's Hill, June 17, 1775.

Archibald Willard,
The Spirit of '76.

The battle between the British and the American revolutionary army in Boston, June 17, 1775, marked the outbreak of the War of Independence. Trumbull, son of the Governor of Connecticut and an officer of the Continental Army of the rebel colonies, subsequently studied under Benjamin West in London and became a professional artist. This picture [OPPOSITE], a deliberate attempt to mythologize the revolution, has become one of the most important social and artistic documents of American life.

This [ABOVE], the most celebrated of all artistic documents of the American Revolution, is the work of a nineteenth-century commercial artist. Frankly propagandistic, it triumphantly encapsulates the "Yankee Doodle" theme of American nationalism.

A loud murmur rose from the street through the open window. At the same moment, something magnetic, not to be put into words, yet very definite, passed through each of us....

"It's come."

"Yes," nodded Le Mée, "it has come." We ran to the window. Down below in the street, moving towards the barracks, we saw a rolling wave of heads. Every face wore the same expression of blank stupor and distraction; in all the eyes was the same strange phosphorescent gleam. There came a hoarse strangled sound of women's voices.

"Well, Le Mée, here's health to you. And may we crack a bottle again together a few months hence."

"Here's to us."

And picking up our swords we ran back to barracks.

Paul Lintier, a French gunner, on the outbreak of the First World War.

Peter Paul Rubens, *Marie de Medici*.

Hyacinthe Rigaud,
Philip V of Spain.

This portrait of Marie de Medici [OPPOSITE], Queen Mother and Regent of France, was painted for the Palais du Luxembourg. Commissioned during the Thirty Years' War, it represents the queen as a goddess of war, perhaps Bellona, surrounded by military impedimenta of the period and crowned with victory laurels.

This official portrait by Louis XIV's principal court artist [ABOVE] depicts the king's second grandson, Philip of Anjou, as King of Spain. His succession to the Spanish throne, which threatened the contemporary balance of power in Europe, was the occasion of the outbreak of the War of the Spanish Succession.

III
Heroes & Leaders

Edmund Dulac, *Poland, A Nation* from *Efforts and Ideals*.

Gliding up the St. Lawrence at the head of the force he was leading in a river assault on the defenses of Quebec, James Wolfe was heard by his staff to murmur a few lines of Gray's *Elegy in a Country Churchyard* and then to remark that he would rather have written the poem than win the honor of capturing the city. Within a few hours he was dead. If he is now as well remembered as the poet he admired, it is perhaps as much for the character that sentiment revealed as for his posthumous victory. For the hero is more often the stuff of literature than its devotee, and his necessary qualities different from and much less attractive then the lyric sensitivity of Wolfe.

Yet heroism and literature are inextricably intertwined, in part because of the notorious fascination of the man of action for the man of ideas, in part because without celebration – in metal, marble, paint but above all in words – heroism fails for lack of an audience. By no one is that truth better understood than the hero – particularly the would-be hero – himself. In the ancient world, emperors, kings and conquerors caused their own exploits to be celebrated on a literally monumental scale ("My name is Ozymandias, King of Kings/Look on my works, ye mighty, and despair"), and the works they created survive in many cases to this day, scarcely diminished by time or the elements. Their modern imitators, liberated from the check to human immodesty imposed by the medieval church, have resumed the habit, creating in the process styles which epitomize the times they dominated: Condottiere Classical, Habsburg Baroque, First Empire, Nuremberg Rally, Stalinoid Brutalist. But architectural self-advertisement, for all its durability lacks the sublime power to inspire which words convey, and those who seek to perpetuate a heroic tradition or to rear the young in its ethos have always recognized the difference. Hence the common institution of the court poet and the royal historiographer; hence, too, the abundance of official biography, written if necessary, as Caesar thought it, by the

Dulac, like his contemporary, Arthur Rackham, was best known for his fantastic illustrations of children's books. But he also did official work, in the design of stamps and banknotes, and during the First World War produced propaganda material for the British government. This illustration was distributed by the Stationery Office and sold both to raise funds for the war effort and to popularize the aims of official war policy. It was also designed to appeal to the national sentiment of Poles in America. The re-establishment of a Polish state became official Allied policy late in the war, and the figure represents a Polish warrior of the sixteenth century, wearing the distinctive feathered wings of the Polish cavalryman of the period, with the Polish white eagle in the background.

subject himself; hence, above all, because to no other theme does the popular poet so readily warm, the universality of the epic poem.

Epics partake of myth as much as of fact, and in that lies a great deal of their power. Perhaps not even the simplest Greeks really believed in the Nemean Lion, the Hydra or the Stymphalian Birds, but it fortified their own courage in the face of ordinary human enemies to think that Hercules had met and killed such monsters. Equally they may have doubted the existence of the one-eyed giant Polyphemus, but the trickery employed by Odysseus to escape his cave must have spurred their imagination and helped sharpen it for use when they found themselves in a tight spot. The most sophisticated of their fellow-countrymen, the teachers of the upper class in republican Athens, though their doubts about the strict veracity of the *Odyssey* and the *Iliad* must have been very strong, made deliberate use of the heroic elements in the poems as models of behavior to the next generation of rulers. And in the same way the *chansons de geste*, in particular the *Song of Roland*, were made the staple of the Christian knight's education in medieval Europe and the principal reference point for his sense of honor. "See, death comes upon us," says Roland to Oliver in the pass of Roncesvalles, "but as noble men we prefer to die by fighting." Exactly that sentiment inspired the crusaders of the *Chanson d'Antioche*, an epic rooted in historical fact, who felt that "it would be better for every man to lose his head than flee even half a foot before the heathen."

It was an important reinforcement of the crusaders' heroic code that they were able to characterize their enemies as morally repugnant because religiously infidel, a mode of thought not open to the pantheistic Greeks, who had in consequence to represent theirs as monstrous or inhuman (though some of Christian Europe's tormentors, like Genghis Khan, appear inhuman to this day, though no doubt seen differently by their own people in their own time). All the more powerful was that reinforcement when integrated with chivalric respect for femininity. Mobilized to inspire a knight's prowess in the tournament or on the field of battle by way of a vow of service to a lady, it affected the final refinement of the heroic ideal. Embodied, as by Joan of Arc, in the person of a real woman, it transformed the use of arms into an almost mystical activity, directed by the voice of God speaking through the virgin he had chosen to lead her followers to victory. Joan is unique; she has no counterpart in Western military history. But her exemplification of the imaginative hold a woman caparisoned for combat could exert on the minds of male warriors may well have underlain the practice, adopted by successive sovereign queens, Elizabeth I of England foremost among them, of affecting military costume and placing themselves symbolically at the head of their armies on the eve of war. We can certainly see that the impact of Florence Nightingale's decision to transvalue the status of the nursing profession derives from her deliberate location of herself and her hospital in the heart of a fighting army, at a time when no respectable women had any association with soldiers except that of marriage. Her title of heroine is indeed in some way a dilution of that of Joan the Virgin's.

Heroism, whether masculine or feminine, is ultimately, however, of limited usefulness on the battlefield, and even its most powerful verbal celebration of limited effect. For in the midst of fear, which is the fighting man's psychological element, it is example which counts. Once armies, and therefore battlefields, grew to a size larger than the individual's eye could take in at a single sweep, heroic behavior lost its power to inspire the mass. The onset of that trend was already perceived by the Greeks in the fifth century B.C., when Xenophon thought it worth rehearsing for himself and his readers the relative merits of rashness and prudence in a commander's behavior. He concluded that rashness was still the more desirable trait. But two hundred years later Philo of Byzantium no longer thought the issue worth debating. "It is your duty," he wrote to an imaginary general, "not to take part in the battle, for whatever you may accomplish by spilling your own blood could not compare with the harm you would do to your own interests if anything happened to you...keeping yourself out of range of missiles, or moving along the lines without exposing yourself, exhort the soldiers, distribute praise and honours to those who prove their courage and berate and punish the cowards."

In this short passage, Philo sums up almost all the duties of the commander as we recognize them today. Only those of planning the campaign — "strategy" — and manoeuvring his army to battle on favorable terms by "stratagem" — both words which nevertheless derive from the Greek for "general" — are omitted. Philo's commander, in short, has become a manager of heroes, rather than a hero himself (though he may have won that reputation in youth), a man who "leads" from behind. The art of leadership from the rear is quite different from the impulse to heroic display, requiring both training and experience to master. And in the great military civilization of Rome, within which the Greek world has eventually subsumed, the public life of the upper class was so organized as to lead the young aristocrat through all the necessary stages. Apprenticed as a junior officer in a legion, he moved, if merit took him that way, via its command into politics and perhaps eventually to leadership of the republic. Realistically the Romans accepted the total interdependence of force and persuasion in the government of men. It was only when the republic succumbed to dynastic and imperial rule that the system, increasingly dependent on the one hand on professional civil servants, gave birth on the other to career generals. Too often the more successful took the empire for themselves, but after its collapse in the west, the eastern half produced at least one great commander of the wholly modern professional type in Belisarius.

In the chaotic kingdoms of post-Roman Europe, heroism and leadership became once more intertwined, both in the minds of the ruling class and their subjects, and would remain so in many states almost into our own times. Three of Germany's seven armies were mobilized in 1914 under the command of royal princes, and both the Kaiser and the Czar thought it necessary to spend the whole war at general headquarters. Yet paradoxically the office and role of the career general was by then firmly institutionalized in the western world, and had been for several centuries. The origin of that development lay in the proprietorship of the mercenary companies which had come to dominate military life at the end of the Middle Ages. Many of these proprietors — *condottieri* — used their skills to become rulers in their own right — the Medici of Florence were almost an exception to that trend — but despite the danger implicit in the transaction, others found for theirs a ready market in the service of established ruling houses. Their example also acted as a spur to subject noblemen, the more ambitious of whom, recognizing that the days of mere heroism were over, sought to emulate their professionalism. Among the first and greatest was Isabella and Ferdinand of Spain's "Gran Capitan," Gonsalo de Cordoba who, beginning as a minor courtier, virtually created the Spanish Army and yet ended his life as he had begun it, a loyal subject. The pattern was reinforced by the career of Philip II's general, the Duke of Parma, Henry IV of France's opponent in the Netherlands. But truer to an older tradition, his life was ended by wounds received in battle.

Under such great military servants of the European crowns, a whole new range of opportunity for permanent, salaried employment opened to the minor aristocracies, an alternative to the scarce "offices" at court from which they were excluded by the greater families. Military office produced the career of "officer," which soon came to have its own internationally recognized hierarchy of steps. Derived from those of the mercenary companies — headman or captain and his deputy or lieutenant — the ladder was extended to include the commander of a column (*colonello*) when companies were so grouped under the "regiment" of royal authority. The grouping of regiments into a field army required that these ranks be made "general" over it; hence (captain-) general, lieutenant-general and, from the senior common soldier of the old company, (sergeant-) major-general. The hierarchy was conventionally crowned by the royal appointment of marshal, called "field" to distinguish him from the civil marshals of the court.

We find most of these ranks in use in the armies of the Civil War in England, and all, including that of marshal, in those of Louis XIV; Peter the Great carefully copied them for the royal army he created on western lines in Russia. We do not, however, find any organized method of appointing men to, let alone training them for, these ranks until much later. The heroic ideal still gripped the old warrior class strongly enough to ensure rejection of the demeaning notion that its siblings needed to be taught how to behave on a battlefield. And the first military academies were indeed established for precisely those branches of soldiering which aristocrats would not practice: fortification and gunnery. The most to which they would consent was genteel education in military boarding schools, where instruction was specifically not military in scope. It was in one of these, at Brienne, that Napoleon began his service life.

Yet within a hundred years of Louis XIV's death, the modern military academies had everywhere come into being: Sandhurst (1799), West Point (1803), St. Cyr (1801), the latter a creation of Napoleon's. Very shortly afterward, a secondary tier was added. In 1810, Prussia founded a War Academy to teach these skills not to future lieutenants but to future generals, and by the end of the nineteenth century "command staff colleges" flourished in all advanced countries. Their aim, moreover, was to produce a soldier whom Xenophon might have had difficulty in recognizing as a fellow-practitioner of the art, and to whom Bohemond or even Napoleon's swashbuckling Marshal Murat would have denied the title of warrior altogether. A creature of the study and the map room, his skills lay in the understanding of the science of military movement and supply, and in the laying of plans to be executed far from the sound of gunfire. Planning and logistics had increasingly taken hold of the military mind, of course, as armies had grown in numbers from thousands toward millions. Yet Alexander the Great, a considerable logistician, had nevertheless thought his proper place in the battle line and Napoleon had, as a young commander, frequently and ostentatiously risked his life. The new breed, of whom Ulysses Grant of the American Union Army represents an early type, took up position elsewhere, very often near a railway and at the end of a telegraph line, which now provided the chief means of controlling armies so widely scattered that not even a man on a good horse could visit all units in a single day. By the end of the nineteenth century, the trend had become so exaggerated that the German Great General Staff, model for all others in the contemporary military world, could be commanded by a man who made a fetish of his seclusion and intellectuality, very rarely leaving his office to visit troops even in the depths of the great European peace. Schlieffen had his foreign counterparts – Pétain in France, Kitchener in England – and it was to be their peculiar fate to seek counter-plans to his own, posthumously bequeathed to the German Army, when the First World War, which it largely precipitated, broke out.

The cult of detachment reached its apogee in that conflict, during which the vast majority of the soldiers who suffered and died at the behest of the high command never once set eyes on the men who gave the orders. The result was an effusion, some ten years after the Armistice, of bitterly anti-military literature, aimed both at the iron face of war itself and at the flint-hearted technocrats who worked its levers by remote control. But alienation from those anti-heroes was not confined to the mind of civilians and ex-soldiers. The younger generation of officers had also reacted violently against the château generalship of 1914-18 and determined that, in any future conflict, their style of command would be different. And so in the Second World War it proved to be. Generalship once again become conspicuous, as commanders strove to show themselves to the troops at the front lines, at or near which it became the fashion to establish headquarters. Montgomery commanded from a mobile trailer, Rommel and Guderian from radio trucks which manoeuvred behind the leading tanks. The result was a sharp rise in fatalities among the higher ranks, but also a renewed confidence in their leaders among ordinary soldiers and a return of something like heroic status to the most bold and successful of them. Those who benefited most from this revived regard were the guerrilla generals, whose lives were lived at the frontiers of danger and who shared to the full the hardships of their followers. T. E. Lawrence, almost alone among First World War leaders, had assured a hero's reputation for himself by his brilliant literary narrative of his guerrilla exploits at the head of an Arab army on the Turkish front. In the Second World War, regular soldiers like Wingate, Stilwell and Stirling, whose operations were conducted behind enemy lines and who cultivated a deliberately tough and adventurous style, evoked the same admiring response from their men and the newspaper-reading public. Even more so the nationalist guerrilla leaders, Tito foremost among them, whose resistance to enemy occupation of the homeland took on the character of a true epic and established the post-war politics of their liberated nations on a high romantic plane.

But Tito was, of course, as much a revolutionary as a soldier. And, like the greatest revolutionary leader of the century, Lenin, he intuitively understood the interconnection between personal risk-taking and political credibility. It was that perception which, in an earlier or simpler political world, had emboldened the ambitious to seek the hero's crown on the battlefield, since with it came command in peace as well as war. The modern bourgeois states have been able to dispense with the heroic impulse, for they have succeeded in transferring politics to a level where policy counts for more than personality. By contrast, those among their generals, and particularly the group which planned and directed that great cataclysm of bourgeois states, the First World War, had to learn the hard way that in the leadership of armies there is no substitute for heroism. Victories won without it are bought with the blood of disillusioned men, partake of the moral atmosphere of defeat and inspire the bitter reproaches of all — historians, poets or mere survivors — who contemplate the aftermath.

Little Sir Thomas Morgan, the great soldier, was of meane Parentage in Monmouthshire. He went over to the Lowe-Countrie warres about 16, being recommended by some friend of his to some Commander there, who, when he read the letter, sayd, What! has my cosen recommended a *Rattoon* to me? at which he tooke pett, and seek't his fortunate (as a soldier) in Saxon Weymar.

He spake Welch, English, French, High Dutch, and Low Dutch, but never a one well. He seated himself at Cheuston, in Herefordshire.

Sir John Lenthall told me at the taking of Dunkyrke, Marshall Turenne, and, I thinke, Cardinall Mezarine too, had a great mind to see this famous Warrior. They gave him a visitt, and wheras they thought to have found an Achillean or gigantieque person, they saw a little man, not many degrees above a dwarfe, sitting in a hutt of Turves, with his fellowe soldiers, smoaking a Pipe about 3 inches (or neer so) long, and did cry-out to the Soldiers, when angry with them, *Sirrah, I'le cleave your skull!* as if the wordes had been prolated by an Eunuch.

John Aubrey,
Brief Lives, circa 1650

Kimon Evan Marengo, *The Progress of Russian and German Cooperation, 1940.*

A member of the Egyptian European community, Marengo was much employed by the British Ministry of Information during the Second World War to produce anti-Axis cartoons for the Arab world. This example dates from the period of the Russo-German alliance, September, 1939 to June, 1941.

Sir Herbert von Herkomer and F. Goodall, *Earl Kitchener of Khartoum*.

Kitchener, an officer of the Royal Engineers, became the most successful of Britain's late nineteenth-century imperial campaigners. In 1898 he completed the recapture of the Sudan at the head of an Anglo-Egyptian army (this portrait [LEFT] has the walls and minarets of Khartoum as its background), in 1902 brought the Boer War to an end, and in 1914 was appointed Secretary of State for War on the outbreak of the First World War. He was drowned while on a voyage to Russia in 1916. Although then regarded by his colleagues as a failure, he remained a towering popular hero.

This print [ABOVE] by an anonymous cartoonist probably dates from 1827, when Wellington succeeded the Duke of York as Commander-in-Chief. On the heel of the boot is a spur bearing the abbreviations of his principal honors: Knight of the Garter and Grand Cross of the Orders of the Bath and Hanover. The building in the background is the Horseguards, Whitehall, headquarters of the army.

James McBey, *Lawrence of Arabia*.

Stefano Torelli, *Catherine the Great*.

McBey was a British Official War Artist, sent to paint in the Middle Eastern theatre. This portrait [ABOVE LEFT], done in Damascus in October, 1918, is of particular interest because it dates from the period immediately before the outbreak of Lawrence's great fame. The romantic style and expression, which exactly capture what a contemporary called Lawrence's genius for "backing into the limelight," no doubt subsequently contributed to Lawrence's renown.

This state portrait [ABOVE RIGHT], by one of the immigrant artists who supplied the St. Petersburg court with its fashionable trappings, perfectly captures the strength of character and self-satisfaction of the minor German princess who, after deposing her husband, ruled triumphantly in his stead as a conquering empress.

V. Kamenski, *Lenin*.

Francisco Goya, *General Antonio de Ricardos*.

This government poster [ABOVE LEFT], celebrating the anniversary of the October Revolution, represents Lenin in a heroic guise characteristic of early Soviet art. The slogan reads, "Long Live the Socialist Revolution," and the background depicts stylized episodes of the events of October, 1917.

This complacent portrait [ABOVE RIGHT], which dates from the artist's time as principal painter to the Spanish court, depicts one of the myriad generals of the top-heavy Spanish army of the eighteenth century. Their ineffectuality in the face of Napoleon's invasion was a main cause of the popular revolt of 1808.

George Catlin, *Crow Warrior.*

Catlin was one of several American artists who sought to document the landscape and native life of the American frontier during the great westward movement of the nineteenth century. He was best known for his paintings of Indians, whose warrior ferocity excited a romantic fascination in stay-at-home Americans of the period [ABOVE].

The most famous glorification of Napoleon by his favorite artist, this triumphal canvas [OPPOSITE] shows him, as First Consul, crossing the Great St. Bernard on his way to victory over the Austrians at Marengo in 1800. The composition deliberately alludes to the struggle of Alexander with his horse, Bucephalus. And, to emphasize the theme of conquest, Bonaparte's name has been boldly inscribed on the rocks of the pass above those of others who had passed that way: Hannibal and Charlemagne.

Jean-Louis David, *Napoleon Crossing the Alps*.

The King dismounted and stood leaning
against his saddle; around him were his
familiar knights, Geoffrey of Sargines,
John Foinon, John of Valéry, Peter of
Bauçay, Robert of Bazoches and Walter of
Châtillon, who, seeing that his illness
had grown worse and that he was exposing himself to peril by staying on land,
began all together, and each one
separately, to beg him to save his life by
boarding a ship. He continued to refuse
to abandon his people; King Charles, his
brother, then Count of Anjou, said to
him: "Sire, you do ill to resist the good
advice that your friends give you, and to
refuse to embark on a ship; for by waiting for you on land, the march of the
army is delayed, not without danger,
and you might be the cause of our loss."
He said that, as he reported later, out of a
desire to save the King, fearing so greatly
to lose him, when he would gladly have
given his whole inheritance and that of
his children to have the King in
Damietta. But the King, deeply upset,
answered him with a wrathful look:
"Count of Anjou, Count of Anjou! If I am
a burden to you, rid yourself of me; but I
will never rid myself of my people."

*St. Louis, King of France,
at Damietta, April 6, 1250.*

Kiyohiro, *Yoshitune*.

Engraving, *The Duke of Parma*.

H.A. Ogden, *Grant in the Wilderness*.

The figure Yoshitune was a real historical person of the twelfth century, who became a legendary hero of Japan [OPPOSITE].

Alexander Farnese [ABOVE LEFT], Third Duke of Parma (1545-92), was Philip II of Spain's principal general in Philip's war against his rebellious subjects in the Netherlands. A soldier of towering ability, Farnese came near to subduing the rebellion but was eventually defeated by his master's insistence on his intervening in the French wars of religion before the Dutch Protestants had been beaten.

This popular magazine-style lithograph [ABOVE RIGHT] shows an uncharacteristically benign Ulysses S. Grant, Commander-in-Chief of the Union armies, during the Battle of the Wilderness, May 5-6, 1864. A resolute strategic realist, Grant transformed the North's conduct of the war against the South. The Battle of the Wilderness was the first of his steps to encircle the southern capital of Richmond and drive Lee's army into the interior.

The first thing I did, of course, was to put out my hand and congratulate him upon his victory. He made a variety of observations in his short, natural, blunt way, but with the greatest gravity all the time, and without the least approach to anything like triumph or joy. – "It has been a damned serious business," he said. "Blücher and I have lost 30,000 men. It has been a damned nice thing – the nearest run thing you ever saw in your life. Blücher lost 14,000 on Friday night, and got so damnably licked I could not find him on Saturday morning; so I was obliged to fall back to keep up my communications with him." – Then, as he walked about, he praised greatly those Guards who kept the farm (meaning Hugomont) against the repeated attacks of the French; and then he praised all our troops, uttering repeated expressions of astonishment at our men's courage. He repeated so often its being *so nice a thing – so nearly run a thing*.

Thomas Creevey visits the Duke of Wellington the morning after Waterloo.

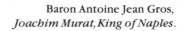

Baron Antoine Jean Gros, *Joachim Murat, King of Naples*.

The son of an inn-keeper and a former private soldier of the royal army, Murat was one of nature's *beaux sabreurs* to whose talents the Revolution opened a career. His dash as a cavalry leader endeared him to Napoleon, who gave him the throne of Naples as a reward for his exploits on the battlefield. Murat never lost his juvenile taste for the tawdry; for his portrait by one of the leading official artists of the Empire, he has donned a Marshal's coat, a lancer's cap, the tiger skin shabraque of the Guard Hussars, the sash and star of the Legion of Honor, and feathers to taste.

Tosa Mitsuyoshi, *The Battle of the Uji River* (detail).

Twelfth-century Japan was rent by civil wars between the samurai clans, which culminated in the victory of the Minamoto and their acquisition of supreme power under the emperor of Shoguns. This dramatic painting is of an episode in the Uji River battle of 1184.

This representation of the legendary combat between father and son [RIGHT] shows both arrayed in the panoply of Moghul warriors of the period, equipped with quivers of arrows and the powerful composite bow of the Mongols, but fighting with damascene swords.

A child monarch, Peter amused himself as a boy by drilling his companions in regiments whose organization and dress were modeled on that of contemporary Western armies. A coup against him by the traditional military class in 1689 allowed him to establish effective power, when he transformed his toy units into the two premier regiments of the Russian Imperial Guard, the Preobrajensky and Semenowsky. This contemporary illustration [FAR RIGHT] shows the boy king at his war games.

Persian manuscript miniature, *Combat of Sohrab and Rustum*.

Kzekchinine, *Peter the Great and his Infantry Regiments*.

German tapestry, *Joan of Arc at Chinon* (detail).

The peasant girl of Domrémy, self-appointed, or as she believed, God-chosen, savior of France presented herself at the court of the Dauphin in Chinon on February 23, 1429 [ABOVE]. After two days' wait, she was allowed entry and succeeded in convincing him that she could lead the king's armies to victory over the English.

An example of fine Persian art, this image [OPPOSITE] represents the twelfth-century hero of the Mongol world in hand-to-hand combat with his enemies.

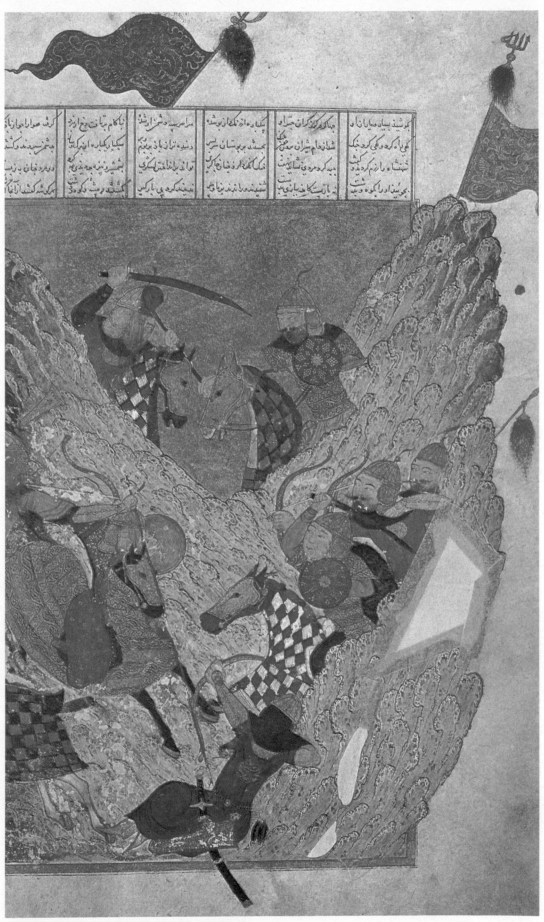

Persian manuscript illumination, *Genghis Khan*.

This canvas [BELOW], from the Medici cycle painted for the Palais du Luxembourg, has as its theme the apotheosis of the assassinated Henry IV, victor of the French wars of religion, and the succession of Marie de Medici as regent to the infant Louis XIV.

This remarkable confection by the leading French Romantic of the early period [OPPOSITE ABOVE] combines several disparate elements with considerable artistic success. The Gaelic poet Ossian, largely the creation of the literary forger James McPherson, receives Napoleon's generals under the Roman eagle while Norse Valkyrie float about his feet, strumming on the instruments used to accompany Greek poetical declamation. It was said that Girodet took "infinite trouble to be original," and perhaps never more so than in this picture, painted as a ceiling for Napoleon's residence at Malmaison.

Better known for his indispensible *Lives of the Artists* than for his own painting, Vasari was a most gifted artist himself. This glorification of the first and perhaps greatest of the Medici [OPPOSITE BELOW] represents him in the traditional guise of a conqueror, although his real talents were for politics and business.

Peter Paul Rubens, *The Apotheosis of Henry IV and the Regency.*

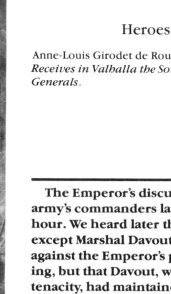

Anne-Louis Girodet de Roucy Trioson, *Ossian Receives in Valhalla the Souls of Napoleon's Generals*.

The Emperor's discussion with the army's commanders lasted for over an hour. We heard later that everyone except Marshal Davout had argued against the Emperor's plan for advancing, but that Davout, with his usual tenacity, had maintained that it was only at Moscow that we could sign a peace treaty, and the result of this conference, which was to have so important an effect on the destiny of France, was the order to depart the next day.

The Emperor mounted his horse, and we entered Smolensk. It was midday. The heat was prostrating. The King of Naples, who had been indisposed for several days, was taken ill, and we carried him to his headquarters where he was obliged to go to bed. At about three o'clock the Emperor sent for him. Murat sent a reply to the effect that he had nothing to add to what he had said in the morning, and that Napoleon could dispose of his life but not make him alter his opinion.

Colonel Marie-Joseph Rosetti's account of Napoleon's conference with his marshals, Smolensk, August 17, 1812.

Giorgio Vasari, *Apotheosis of Cosimo I*.

Benjamin West, *The Death of General Wolfe*.

...I desire that Miss Lowther's picture may be set in jewels to the amount of five hundred guineas, and returned to her.

I leave to Col. Oughton, Col. Carleton, Col. Howe and Col. Warde a thousand pounds each. I desire Admiral Saunders to accept of my light service of Plate, in remembrance of his Guest. My camp equipage, kitchen furniture, table linen, wine and provisions, I leave to the officer who succeeds me in the command.

All my books and papers, both here and in England, I leave to Col. Carleton.

I leave Major Barre, Capt. de Laune, Capt. Smyth, Capt. Bell, Capt. Leslie and Capt. Caldwell each a hundred guineas to buy swords and rings, in remembrance of their friend. My servant François shall have half of my clothes and linen here, and the three footmen shall divide the rest amongst them. All the servants shall be paid their year's wages and their board wages till they arrive in England, or till they engage with other masters, or enter some other profession. Besides this, I leave fifty guineas to François, twenty to Ambrose and ten to each of the others.

Will made by Major-General James Wolfe on the eve of the taking of Quebec and his own death, September 12, 1759.

John Singleton Copley, *The Death of Major Peirson*.

West's commemoration of the death of General James Wolfe in the moment of victory on the Plains of Abraham, September 13, 1759 [OPPOSITE], is important for more than historical reasons. Though by no means a great artist, West here succeeded in inventing a new artistic form by representing a heroic theme in contemporary instead of antique costume. The composition breaks further conventions by imitating the "deposition," the traditional arrangement of figures in pictures of Christ's body being taken down from the cross. The picture, it has been said, expresses "the shift of emotional allegiance from religion to nationalism;" all its elements swiftly found numerous imitators.

This picture [ABOVE] depicts the death of an English major who rallied his troops in St. Helier, Jersey, after the town had been captured by the French and surrendered by the governor. Major Peirson's troops defeated the French, but he died in battle.

As his army was very small in comparison to that of Darius, Alexander took care to draw it up so as to prevent its being surrounded, by stretching out his right wing farther than the enemy's left. In that wing he acted in person, and fighting in the foremost ranks, put the Barbarians to flight. He was wounded, however, in the thigh, and (according to Chares) by Darius, who engaged him hand to hand. But Alexander, in the account he gave of the battle, does not mention who it was that wounded him; he only says he received a wound in his thigh by a sword, and that no dangerous consequences followed it.

The victory was a very signal one, for he killed above a hundred and ten thousand of the enemy. Nothing was wanting to complete it but the taking of Darius, and that prince escaped narrowly, having got the start of his pursuer only by four or five furlongs. Alexander took his chariot and his bow, and returned with them to his Macedonians.

Alexander the Great
at the Battle of Issus in 333 B.C.,
from Plutarch's Lives.

Francisco Goya, *The Maid of Saragossa* from *The Horrors of War*.

Jerry Barret, *Florence Nightingale at Scutari*.

Jean-Louis David, *The Sabine Women Halting the Battle Between the Romans and the Sabines* (detail).

This etching [OPPOSITE ABOVE] from the *Horrors of War* series (1808-20), devoted to the resistance of the Spanish people to Napoleon's invasion, illustrates an incident in the Siege of Saragossa, 1808, when Maria Augustin, "the Maid of Saragossa," continued to serve a gun on the walls after its male crew had been killed around it. This episode is also commemorated in Byron's *Childe Harold*. Goya entitled the work *Que Valor!* (What Courage!).

Florence Nightingale's hospital at Scutari, across the Bosphorus from Constantinople, became the main depot for British sick and wounded soldiers evacuated from the Crimea in 1854-6. It was there, patroling the wards at night, that she achieved immortality as "the Lady with the Lamp." This admirably unromanticized picture [OPPOSITE BELOW] shows her receiving casualties at the main gate of the hospital, a disused Turkish barracks, presumably early in her reign, before she had recovered it from decrepitude.

An entirely imaginary recreation, despite the authenticity of archeological detail, David's battle scene [ABOVE] is chiefly important as a triumph of the neo-classical style, of which he was the unchallenged master, and for its influence on military painting during and after the Napoleonic wars. His followers included Girodet and Gros.

May it please your Most Excellent Majesty; – I have forborne this long time to write unto your Majesty, hoping that the wind would have served that on this I might have certified your Majesty of something worth the writing.

We have often put to the sea with contrary winds; and in the end, not being able to continue out for fear of being driven to the leeward as far as the Wight, were forced in again, into Plymouth. Our victuals were spent, and the wind not serving our vituals to come to us, we expected the goodness of God to change the wind, which did happily change on Friday morning, so that on Saturday, late at night, they came to us. They were no sooner come, although it were night, but we went all to work to get in our victuals, which I hope shall be done in 24 hours, for no man shall sleep or eat till it be despatched; so that, God willing, we will be under sail tomorrow morning, being Monday, and the 24th of this present month. I humbly beseech your Majesty to think that there was never men more unwilling to lose any time than we are....

Lord Howard of Effingham to Queen Elizabeth on setting sail against the Spanish Armada, June 23, 1588.

P. Moreelse, Christian, Hereditary Bishop of Halberstadt.

A younger brother of Duke Frederick Ulrich of Brunswick, Christian became a notable leader of cavalry on the Protestant side during the Thirty Years' War; he has also been called "one of the most brutal condottieri of the war and a foul-mouthed censor of would-be peacemakers." His portraitist has faithfully recorded the costume and accoutrements of a rich soldier of the period. He wears half-armor and carries an expensive wheel-lock pistol.

Unknown, *Elizabeth I*.

One of a number known as the Armada Portraits, this picture shows the queen dressed in the height of French court fashion, one hand resting on an orb which is actually a globe, the other on a sword hilt. The scenes beyond, apparently seen through the stern lights of a warship, show, left, the English fleet bearing down on the crescent formation of the Spanish Armada; right, the Armada's destruction in the great storms that ravaged its homeward journey. These marine scenes are probably a seventeenth-century re-painting.

At this moment a Spanish officer looked over the quarter deck rail and said they surrendered. From this most welcome intelligence it was not long before I was on the quarter deck when the Spanish captain with a bow presented me his sword and said the Admiral was dying of his wounds below. I asked him on his honour if the ship was surrendered. He declared she was, on which I gave him my hand and desired him to call to his officers and ship's company and tell them of it which he did, and on the quarter deck of a Spanish first rate extravagant as the story may seem did I receive the swords of vanquished Spaniards which as I received I gave to William Fearney one of my barge men who put them with the greatest *sang froid* under his arm.

Nelson's letter to his wife describing his taking of the San Josef, *February 14, 1797.*

French lithographic illustration, *A Hygiene Fanatic*.

The French, like the rest of Europe, were strongly critical of Britain's war against the Boers in South Africa (1899-1902), which they regarded as aggressive and imperialist. This satirical illustration from *La France de Bordeaux* shows Sir Redvers Buller urging Sir Charles Warren to cut short his morning bath and engage the enemy at the Battle of Spion Kop, January 23, 1900. Though popular with his soldiers, Buller was an unsuccessful general, and he and Warren made easy figures of fun.

Honoré Daumier, *Joyously Singing, Our Brave Troops Move to the Front*.

The most powerful social satirist of the
nineteenth century, Daumier did not spare
French institutions or personalities when he
found a target, but this lithograph represents
Prussian soldiers.

IV
Campaigns

G. di Ventura, *The Battle of Monteparti* (detail).

Home before the leaves fall," promised the Kaiser to his soldiers as they marched off for Paris in 1914. Even in the twentieth century, a would-be conqueror had to think of the seasons, wait until the grain was gathered when contemplating war, count the weeks before the autumn rains came to bemire his armies, the snow to shiver them into winter quarters. Campaigning still came after a harvest, or early enough in summer to be finished before the fields were ripe for the reapers. Harvests and campaigning went together; one supported the other.

Truly primitive people, we may conclude, did not campaign. The hand-to-mouth life of the gatherer, the hunter's round of his traps and waterholes lent men neither the time nor material surplus to quit the tribe for war in the territory of another. Pastoralists may campaign, if an enemy's territory lies along the grazing line of their herds. But not far beyond the range of their herds' progression, unless it takes them by the cultivated land of richer peoples who may be plundered for sustenance. And people frequently plundered are soon not rich. A few pastoralists, like the Mongol Khans of the Golden Horde, learned the art of milking less warlike neighbors for regular tribute. But most either scorched the surface of cultivated land barren by their depredations or were themselves eventually destroyed by the violent reaction of their victims.

For it is the ultimate strength of agricultural societies that their economy yields the means to feed and support specialized fighting men who, as an army, may take the field – *la campagna* – for longer than any migrant invader can afford to linger. Nor must such armies' operations remain defensive; a natural consequence of successful domestic defense is to carry war to the enemy in a campaign of conquest. Which society first raised a campaigning army we can now only guess. The old Egyptian Kingdom, the Sumerians and the Hittites could all call large bodies of militia – seasonal hosts of warriors – into being. But the Assyrian state was the earliest one we can identify as maintaining a body of soldiers permanently under arms and organizing the trains of supply necessary to sustain it in expeditions against rebellious subject peoples or enemies beyond the frontier. By the eighth century B.C., Tiglath-pileser III commanded an army which in its essential elements – cavalry, infantry, engineers and transport – differed not at all from those of modern

The subject of this detail, taken from a fresco, is the defeat of the Gulephs by the Florentine Ghibellines in 1260.

times. It probably also resembled modern armies in numbering paymasters on its staff, for the Assyrians certainly employed mercenaries, men who serve for money. They also furnished much of the strength of the Assyrians' imperial successors in the Middle East, the Persians. Many of Persia's soldiers were Greeks who had learned their trade in the local wars of the city-states but, denied a living by the chronic shortage of land at home, had been driven abroad to practice their skills. And two centuries after Darius launched his enormous invasion to subjugate Greece, a native Greek army would make the journey in the opposite direction at the outset of an even more dramatic, and on this occasion successful, campaign. Alexander, after conquering all Persia's former possessions, would invade India and resupply himself on his return from a fleet he had established in the Indian Ocean.

The unity of Alexander's empire (336-323 B.C.) was short-lived. But, even while its pieces were being disputed among his generals, the Diadochi, a new imperial power was growing in the Mediterranean. And out of Rome's victories in the Italian peninsula was to rise the greatest campaigning army in history. Initially a militia of the city and surrounding Latium, by the first century A.D. its soldiers had become true long-service regulars, enlisted for twenty years and contracted to serve throughout Rome's possessions. Their military home was the Legion. Six thousand strong, it was trained to march fifteen miles a day and equipped to build itself a secure fortified camp each night. These "marching camps" are found all over the territory of the Empire, from northern Scotland to Egypt, from Portugal to Romania. Their pattern is standard. An earthen wall and ditch encloses space for seven hundred and fifty tents, each holding eight men, pitched around a central headquarters, treasury and grain store. The money and wheat contained therein fueled the legionary machine and through it drove the boundaries of the Empire out to the natural frontiers of the conquered lands. In time, the marching camps became stone fortresses and the routes between them the paved highways of the imperial road system. By the second century, the legions had ceased to conquer and became the border guards of European order.

Impelled westward by a mysterious turbulence in Central Asia — which also shook the security of the world's other walled empire in China — great movements of population collapsed the fixed frontiers of Rome in the fifth century. In its eastern half, Byzantium, a Roman army survived which would retain the power to campaign for almost another thousand years. In the west, regular armies disappeared, to be replaced by the warrior hosts of the Goths or Franks from beyond the Danube or Rhine. These groups not only lacked the discipline to establish stable states but could scarcely hold at bay succeeding waves of ferocious intruders — Moslems from the south, then Vikings from the north and Magyars from the east — which assailed western Europe from the eighth century onward. The crisis ultimately called forth strong new leaders of whom the greatest, the Frankish Charlemagne, declared himself Roman Emperor afresh and founded a novel military system centered on armored horsemen. The knight's mount gave him the mobility to meet intruders at the point of entry, and his mail the protection to make him invincible in battle. The security he gradually restored procured a new economic order in Europe whose purpose was primarily to provide for his maintenance. Called "feudalism" by modern historians, it featured cultivators who depended upon a knight for protection, and whose land was consequently attached to him, which he in turn promised to a greater lord, and ultimately to the King or Holy Roman Emperor, as surety for title. Feudalism promoted a new prosperity and laid the basis for political stability; the states of modern Europe owe their rise to its effects. But feudal warfare, waged over roadless lands and only rarely sustained by proper supply trains, was short in range and limited in object, which often amounted to no more than the settlement of some dynastic quarrel. Of campaigns like those of Alexander or Caesar, it yielded scarcely any example from Charlemagne's expedition into Moslem Spain — the subject of the epic *Song of Roland* — to William of Normandy's Conquest of England in 1066.

The Conquest was not the outcome of chance. The Normans — originally Norsemen, the Vikings of Scandinavia — had learned the art of long-range campaigning in two centuries of expedition and amphibious warfare, which had won them a new land in Iceland, footholds in Britain and Ireland and, via the estuaries of the southern Baltic which they used as highways for their ships, an empire in the interior of modern Russia. In the eleventh century, their ships were to take them as conquerors into the Mediterranean and, in the twelfth, to the Holy Land as the standard-bearers of the Crusades. Amphibious operations were an established feature of Mediterranean warfare, if often as little more than piracy, but also as a principal means of conflict between the opposed empires of Byzantium and Islam, before the Normans' arrival. But the diminution of Moslem power in the western half of the inland sea which the Crusades had brought about prompted the renascent states on its northern shore

— Portugal, Spain and the Italian Cities — to venture westward from its straits toward the lands beyond. So began the era of European world conquest beside which the campaigns of Alexander appear local and tentative.

Its vehicle was the ocean-going sailing ship, large enough to carry both a fighting crew, the food they would consume on a long voyage and even the horses they would ride in battle at their point of debarkation, stout enough to weather the storms of the deep sea and, when the experiment was tried, to stand the shock of discharge of heavy artillery. Its potential was exploited with extraordinary rapidity. Only ten years after Vasco da Gama — himself as much conqueror as explorer — had circumnavigated Africa in 1498, a Portuguese fleet was established in the Indian Ocean and largely controlled its commerce. In 1511, its admiral, Albuquerque, arrived in the East Indies, and by 1542 his successors had sailed as far as Japan. Even more dramatic were the Spanish voyages in the opposite direction. The expedition led by Cortés to Mexico, which used as its starting point the island of Hispaniola where Columbus had made his American landfall in 1492, disposed of only 600 men, 10 cannon and 17 horses. But the fear which those strange animals inspired and the ruthlessness displayed by their riders brought to naught the vastly greater numbers deployed against them by the Aztecs. Ten years later, in 1531, Pisarro's still smaller expedition against the Incas produced the same outcome in Peru. And the military results of the two campaigns did not remain confined to the New World. The enormous wealth in gold and silver which Spanish America yielded returned home to finance the first regular army seen in Europe since the legions and a series of campaigns without parallel in scope or object since Caesar's. On land it paid for the establishment of a strategic highway between Spain's possessions in northern Italy and the Netherlands, which permitted its new army to conduct Mediterranean and continental campaigns simultaneously. At sea it manned and equipped the great fleet sent to invade England in 1588.

Spanish gold proved in practice to have bought the wrong ships for war in northern waters, and the Armada was deflected from England's coasts by the handy, heavily-gunned galleons of Drake and Frobisher. These were to be the prototype of the vessels which would form the lines of battle of all north European navies for the next three centuries, and which were to project British, French and Dutch power to those coasts of the oceans not already colonized by the Spaniards or Portuguese. In the hands of a strategic genius like Nelson, such fleets became the instrument of campaigns conducted across thousands of miles of ocean in the space of weeks, brought to culmination in smashingly decisive off-shore engagements, as at Trafalgar.

But, if Spain was to be eclipsed at sea, her "Spanish Road" in Europe was to prove a military innovation of the greatest significance. Campaigning in the Mediterranean would continue to retain its amphibious character almost into the eighteenth century, so that a great naval victory, like that of the Christian powers over the Ottoman Turks at Lepanto in 1570, is best seen as a land battle between embarked armies. In continental Europe, however, all the rising states attempted to emulate the Spanish system, using the moneys raised by trade and the taxes levied by their emergent bureaucracies to found permanent armies and support them with supply trains and magazines of stores when they departed on campaign. By the early eighteenth century, campaigning might again be conducted at a considerable range from base, as by Marlborough against the Elector of Bavaria in 1704. True, his axis of supply from the Netherlands lay along the course of the Rhine and in practice much food was brought locally rather than transported in his convoys. But the trend his method exemplified was toward military self-sufficiency, in contrast to the practice of daily foraging which, usually unsweetened by payment, had supported campaigning for a millennium. And even Napoleon, though ruthlessly prepared to live off the country when pressed for time, as on his march to Moscow in 1812, or when unreasonably opposed as he believed himself to be during his long drawn out war in Spain, would organize supply columns when foraging threatened to fail.

Napoleon indeed looked firmly forward, even if we may see that it was the recently improved European road system of which his conquests gave him free use which allowed him to do so. The supplementation of roads with railways, already forming a dense network thirty years after his death, would realize the practice he anticipated. Nineteenth century wars, those of Prussia in Europe and of North and South in the United States, were indeed wars of railways, their routes determining where the lines of advance would run, but also encouraging a scale and duration of campaign never before attempted. Napoleon's armies had numbered hundreds of thousands, and they covered ground at a foot's pace. Those of the Union and Confederacy totaled millions while their elements could be transported hundreds of miles in the course of a week. By 1914, war would become a matter of timetables, with the entire fit male population of a country deployed to the national frontiers within days of the outbreak of war and supported there with food and supplies which arrived as steadily and regularly as at retail outlets in peacetime.

But the application of steam power to military purposes had limitations. Steam navies, which required frequent refueling, proved initially to be shorter in range than sail navies, which were restricted in their sea-keeping only by the quantity of water, salt beef and biscuit embarked. Not until the technique of refueling at sea, pioneered by the American and Japanese navies, was perfected in the Second World War, were naval campaigns again to equal in reach those conducted by Drake or Anson. The only long-range naval expedition fueled by coal, Russia's transferral of her Baltic Fleet to the Pacific in 1904-5, encountered nearly insuperable supply difficulties and culminated in crushing defeat at the hands of the Japanese at the battle of Tsushima.

Steam was also of restricted usefulness in land warfare. For all that it multiplied the size of armies available to the general, powered factory output of weapons and munitions in quantities unmatched before, won food surpluses larger than any yet produced and permitted its preservation in a form highly convenient for campaigning, it could not move armies beyond the "railhead," as strategists came to call the point where railways stopped. Hence, in large measure the extraordinarily static nature of the First World War, in which railways provided the means – millions of tons of ammunition and thousands of miles of barbed wire – toward impermeable defenses, but none of the mobility on the battlefield necessary to break through the fronts so formed. It would take an alternative source of mechanical power, the internal combustion engine, to restore mobility to armies. Mounted in an armored shell and transporting its own heavy gun, it would, as the tank, provide the force necessary to crack fixed defenses and thereafter devastate the lines of supply along which the enemy sustained himself. In the early days of its use, in France in 1940 or Russia in 1941, the tank would indeed range across the theaters of war with a freedom of movement and decisive effect which suggested something of the shock imposed on the settled world by the irruptions of the Mongols. And although armored forces would ultimately, by their multiplication, effectively stalemate each other, the *tours de force* of their early appearance left memories which continued to electrify the military mind and would occasionally break out in brilliant campaigning display, as in the Middle East after 1945.

As the means which at last lent man wings, the internal combustion engine also transformed war in another dimension. The advantages of observation offered by the balloon had been recognized early by armies, and they were quick to seize upon the airplane as a potential weapon. In the First World War, it served chiefly to supply or deny intelligence in the field. In the Second, it provided the means to transport fighting troops rapidly over great distances, sometimes to land them at points of critical importance by parachute and everywhere to visit destruction on the earthbound forces tussling below. As an extension of the striking power of navies, it fought battles on their behalf, often, as at Midway in the Pacific in 1942, of war-winning importance. As the eyes of the fleet, it did much to nullify the revolutionary effect of the submarine on naval campaigning. Eventually, when organized into the great bomber forces launched against each other by the Axis and the Allies, it was used to wage campaigns on its own account, called "strategic" because directed against the factories which fed the armies and navies, the civilian population which manned them, the railways which moved the material between "home front" and the fighting line and the sources of fuel – coal and oil – which drove the engines of war.

The final twist to strategic bombing would be given when chemical defoliant was added to the range of weapons which airplanes might rain down from the skies. Used against the guerrillas' forest bases in Vietnam, it caused the leaves to fall at a general's whim, demonstrating the terrifying mastery over nature, the seasons and the elements which has come to characterize campaigning in the late twentieth century.

Saturday the 26 of August we advanced to a town six miles beyond Uxbridge called Chaffan, where we were quartered that night; at this town a soldier belonging to Lieutenant Colonel Tompson was accidentally slain by shooting off a musket by one of his fellow soldiers, though at a great distance from him, yet shot him in the head whereof he died.

Sabbath day 27 August, we advanced from Chaffan near to a village called Chessun; this day the blue regiment of the trained bands, and the three regiments of the auxiliary forces met us upon a great common about three miles from Chessun, our whole regiment was quartered at one Mr. Cheyney's house, an esquire, where we were well accommodated for beer, having great plenty, two or three hundred of us this night lay in one barne.

Sergeant Henry Foster on the March of the Trained Bands from London, 1642, to join the Parliamentary Army.

Sebastian Vrancz, *Camp Scene* (detail).

A highly convincing documentary painting of the contemporary military scene, perhaps of a mercenary company on campaign in Germany during the Thirty Years' War. In the center the captain of the company, wearing half-armor, confers with his officers, while his trumpeter waits to signal the resulting orders. In the background the rest of the company is entertained by two cavalrymen schooling their horse.

Edouard Detaille, *An Infantry Regiment Halts for Review in the Bois de Boulogne* (detail).

Detaille, with Meissonier and de Neuville, specialized in meticulous documentation of the military scene, past and present; he and de Neuville worked with great success as war artists during the Franco-Prussian War. This peacetime picture shows an infantry regiment waiting to go on parade, perhaps for the *Fête nationale* of July 14, officially established in 1880. In the center the colonel and his officers are visited by the brigadier and his staff, which again includes a trumpeter.

We heard the pipers of the Camerons of Canada and knew that we had not far to go. Then there was a loud bang and Danny fell down with a groan.

"Everybody stand still exactly where you are," I shouted, for it was obviously a *schu*-mine. "Danny, how bad is it?"

I knew it was either a broken ankle or the whole foot blown off — what the doctors call traumatic amputation. Danny's language and Porter, who at great personal risk stepped two or three paces over to him and applied a first field-dressing, told me that it was not too bad. We shouted at the tops of our voices to the Canadians for pioneers with mine-prodders and stretcher-bearers. I looked around and realized now that we were in a narrow no-man's-land, only fifty yards wide, between the German and Canadian positions. Danny, Porter and I were in the middle of a minefield, but fortunately those behind us were still in the old German diggings, so I told them to go back.

Lieutenant-Colonel Martin Lindsay at the Crossing of the Rhine, Spring, 1945.

Alex Colville, *Infantry Near Nijmegen, Holland.*

Gustave Pierre, *Soldiers Marching Off*.

Jan Ditle deBry, after Titian, *A Procession of Prisoners* from *The Greatness of Spain*.

From the series entitled *The Greatness of Spain*, this scene [ABOVE LEFT] is of a sixteenth-century military column on the march. Behind the covered wagon a knot of Moorish prisoners is driven along by guards; the camel is also Moorish booty.

Colville, a Canadian, practiced in the "magic realist" style. He was appointed an Official War Artist and this scene [OPPOSITE] is of Canadian infantry in Holland marching along a dike through flooded country in the harsh winter of 1944-5. The war had become static after the headlong advances of the late summer and autumn, and the men's expressions reflect the dreary state into which the campaign had fallen.

Pierre's picture [ABOVE RIGHT] captures both the appearance and the mood of the French army in 1917. The *poilus* ("bristly ones") are burdened with the impedimenta that make life in the trenches just bearable; their faces imply that they have almost reached the end of their tether. In May, 1917, more than fifty of the hundred divisions of the French army announced their refusal to continue with offensive operations.

The emperor's entourage [RIGHT] mounted, equipped with sheaves of arrows and the powerful Mongol composite bow, and arrayed behind a banner, closely resembles a Manchu war party of the sort that conquered China in the mid-seventeenth century.

Chinese silk scroll painting, *Imperial Hunting Party in Manchuria* (detail).

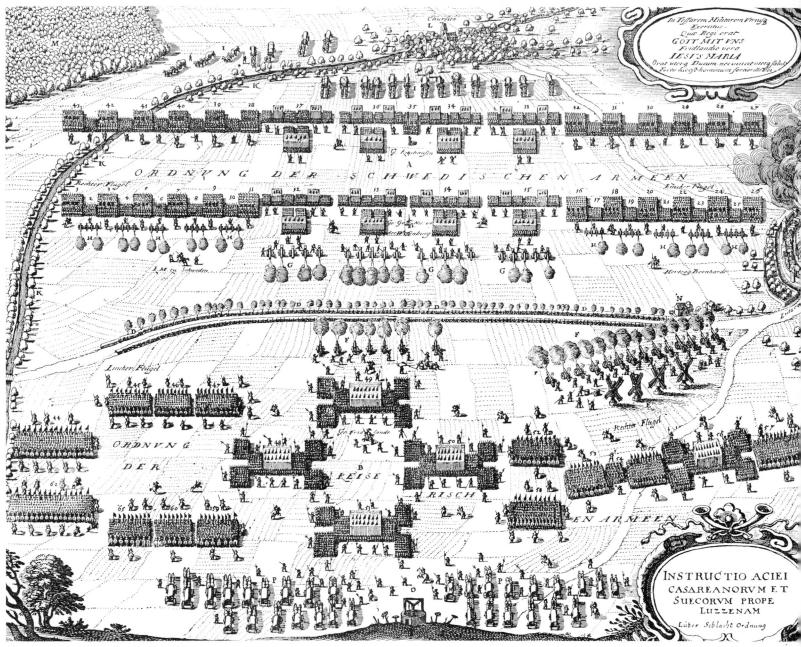

German engraving, *The Battle of Lützen*.

An excellent example of what has been called the "analytical" battle picture [ABOVE], differing from the "narrative," "ornamental" and "glorifying" types in that it attempts to convey the precise organization of the opposing sides and the course of events. The first examples are mid-sixteenth century; by the seventeenth century it had become a recognized and distinct art form to which engineer officers and specialized schools of engravers devoted themselves. This shows the deployment of the Imperial and Swedish armies at Lützen, November 16, 1632, one of the key engagements of the Thirty Years' War. Although a Swedish victory, King Gustavus Adolphus was killed on the field, a grave setback to the Protestant cause.

Napoleon's invasion of Egypt in 1798 drew into Syria a Turkish army under the Sultan's general, Achmed Pasha. Napoleon marched to meet him and, during March and April, 1799, fought a series of engagements. This dramatic canvas [OPPOSITE ABOVE] depicts a clash near Nazareth on April 4; a deliberately romantic composition, it provides in no sense a realistic picture of events.

Simpson, a professional lithographer, went to the Crimea at the outbreak of the war in 1854. From sketches made on the spot he produced a magnificent series of eighty topographical and analytical views of the war, *The Seat of War in the East*, published by Colnaghi and later used as an accompaniment to Kinglake's *History*. This view [OPPOSITE BELOW], drawn within three weeks of the battle of Balaclava (October 25, 1854) and approved by Lord Cardigan, shows the general at the head of his light cavalry, just about to reach the Russian guns.

Baron Antoine Jean Gros,
The Battle of Nazareth.

William Simpson, *The Charge of the Light Brigade* (detail).

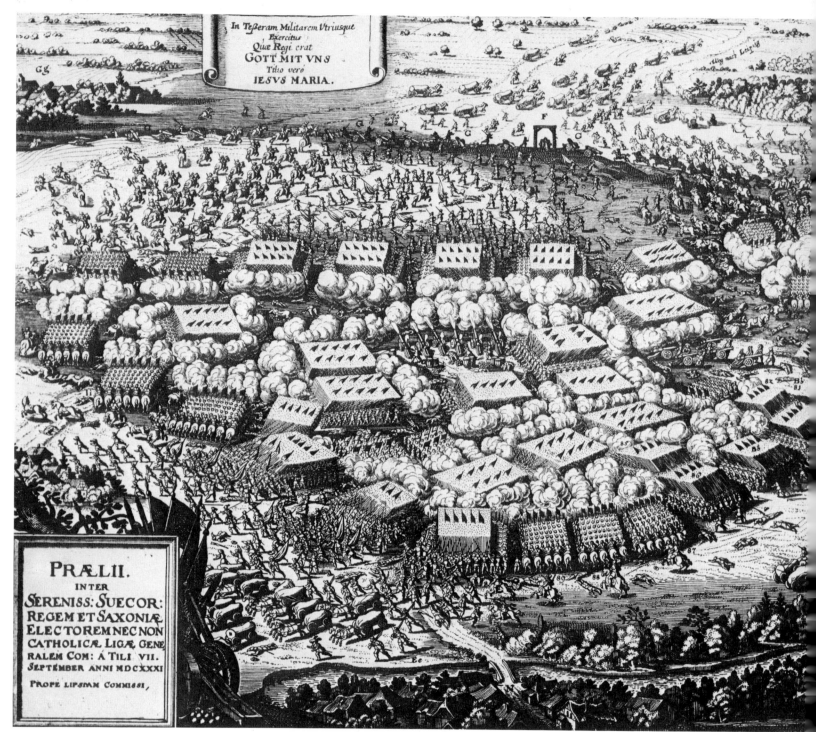

In Tesseram Militarem Vtriusque
Exercitus
Quæ Regi erat
GOTT MIT VNS
Tilio vero
IESVS MARIA.

PRÆLII.
INTER
SERENISS: SUECOR:
REGEM ET SAXONIÆ
ELECTOREM NEC NON
CATHOLICÆ LIGÆ GENE
RALEM COM: À TILI VII.
SEPTEMBER ANNI MDCXXXI
PROPE LIPSIAM COMMISSI,

Mattheus Marain the Elder, *The Battle of
Breitenfeld*.

Indian manuscript illustration (reproduction),
Combat Between Arjuna and Kama.

St. Gallo book painter, Carolingian siege.

Breitenfeld, fought on September 17, 1631, was a brilliant victory by King Gustavus Adolphus of Sweden over the Imperial forces. This "analytical" picture [OPPOSITE] depicts the climactic moment of the battle when Gustavus turned Tilly's flank, top right; the Imperial baggage trail and first fugitives can be seen streaming back toward Leipzig.

An illustration of a Hindu legend, which relates how Arjuna, the son of Indra, shot off the head of Kama, god of love, with an arrow [OPPOSITE BELOW]. Although the subject is traditional, the treatment of the military theme is contemporary and shows Moghul influence.

This whole-page miniature [LEFT] in the Golden Psalter, showing the conquest and surrender of a town, is the most notable work of the late Carolingian St. Gallo book painter.

Solferino, June 24, 1859, was the decisive battle of the war between Austria and the Italian Kingdom, Piedmont, in which France took Piedmont's side. The battle, chiefly an Austro-French affair, resulted in appalling casualties; the neglect of the wounded prompted Dunant to write his *Souvenir de Solferino*, which led to the foundation of the International Red Cross Society. Pettenkofen's impressionistic view of the aftermath [BELOW LEFT] aptly conveys the horror of all massed-rank engagements.

August von Pettenkofen, *Battle of Solferino* (detail).

Elizabeth Southerden
Thompson, *Scotland For
Ever!* (detail).

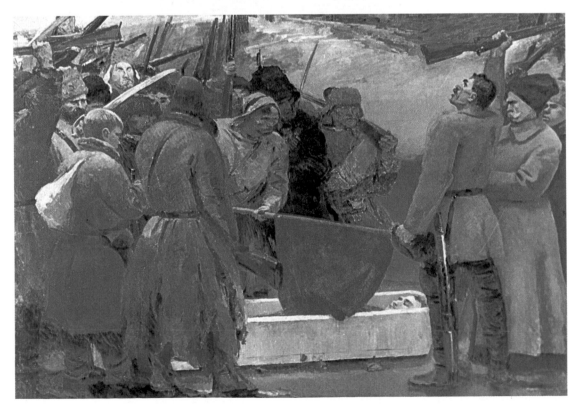

S. Gerasimov, *Oath of
Siberian Guerrillas*.

Thomas Baines, *The Battle of Blauwkrantz*.

This dramatic recreation of the charge of the Royal Scots Greys at Waterloo, June 18, 1815 [OPPOSITE ABOVE] is the work of one of the best-known British military artists of the nineteenth century. Her sister was married to the commanding officer of the Royal Scots Greys at the time she painted the picture, and she was able to arrange for the regiment to charge her at her easel. She succeeded nonetheless in exaggerating the speed and density of the charge.

This Social Realist representation of an incident in the Russian Civil War [OPPOSITE BELOW] is more naturalistic than later developments of the style. Its purpose is nevertheless sternly ideological.

During 1835-7 the fiercely independent Boers of South Africa grew impatient with the restrictions of a British rule in the Cape and trekked north to find free land. This Great Trek brought them into conflict with the Zulus who, before their defeat in the battle of Blood River, December 16, 1838, caught and massacred many of the Boer settler columns. Blauwkrantz was one of these episodes, overdramatized here [ABOVE] by an English popular painter.

When winter with its frosts was over, as soon as the first signs of spring and of softer weather appeared, everyone made ready his horses, arms and baggage and all sent messages inviting each other to set forth. The time of departure of each one was carefully agreed in advance, as were also the meeting-places, and the routes which it would be both safest and easiest for them to take. It would in fact have been impossible for these thousands of travellers to find in every country all that was needful for them; it was therefore carefully arranged that the most notable princes should each separately lead the legions belonging to their suite and take different roads. So it was that their armies were not united until they were in the neighbourhood of Nicaea.

William of Tyre describes the departure of the First Crusade, 1096.

C.H. Vroom, *The Battle of Gibraltar.*

Adriaen van Diest, *Battle of La Hogue*.

An application of the technique of "analytical" battle painting to sea warfare, this canvas [OPPOSITE] depicts the decisive moment of the battle between the Spanish and Dutch fleet, under Admiral Jacob van Heenskerk, off Gibraltar in 1607. The Eighty Years' War between Spain and her Protestant Dutch subjects was fought chiefly in the Netherlands, but the Dutch also carried the war to sea, sometimes far from her shores. Their superiority in oceanic seamanship brought them several successes, of which Gibraltar was the most spectacular.

The decisive sea battle of the War of the Grand Alliance, 1688-97, La Hogue (May 23, 1692) resulted in heavy losses of ships by the French who, despite inferiority of numbers, had attacked the Anglo-Dutch fleet. Diest's painting [ABOVE] is regarded as one of his finest and an excellent example of documentary marine art of the period.

In the most sparkling naval action of the War of the Austrian Succession (May 3, 1747), Admiral Anson intercepted a French convoy, escorted by a squadron under Admiral de la Jonquière, and captured all nine French warships and several of the convoy. The precision and luminosity of Scott's treatment [ABOVE] is characteristic of the work of the van der Veldes, of whom Scott was an imitator.

Russia's high-handed annexation of the Chinese fortress of Port Arthur, Japan's principal prize of her victory over the Chinese in 1895, enraged the Japanese, who in 1904 opened a war against the Russian empire in the Far East by surprise attack. This woodblock print [OPPOSITE ABOVE], one of the last examples of its use for topical purposes, is of Admiral Togo's attack on the Russian battlefleet outside Port Arthur on April 13, 1904. The ship exploding in the left background is the *Petropavlovsk*, flagship of Admiral

Makarov. He went down with it, but his successors lacked his courage and energy and kept the fleet in harbor, where it was eventually destroyed by Japanese land artillery.

One of a convoy attacked by the German pocket battleship *Scheer* in the Atlantic on November 5, 1940, the *San Demetrio* was hit and abandoned by her crew in sinking condition. Next morning one of her lifeboats with thirteen men aboard found her still afloat [OPPOSITE BELOW]. Despite the risk of explosion, they re-boarded, extinguished the fires and brought her, after an eight-day voyage, to the west coast of Ireland. The epic did much to encourage British spirits at a low point of the war. Wilkinson, an Official War Artist in both World Wars (and the inventor of camouflage "dazzle painting" in the First) included the adventure in his *War at Sea* series.

Samuel Scott, *Admiral Anson's Action off Cape Finisterre*.

Kokyo, *Japanese Destroyer Attack at Port Arthur*.

Norman Wilkinson, *Crew Re-boarding the Tanker San Demetrio* from *War at Sea*.

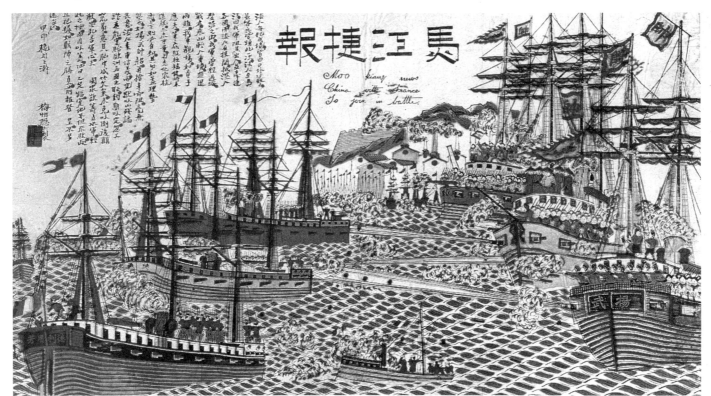

Japanese woodcut, sea fight.

This woodcut [ABOVE] depicts an incident in the Sino-Japanese War of 1894. The French and other European powers were not prepared to allow the Japanese to take part in the grab for Chinese soil and forced Japan to settle for a lesser share than she might have expected.

This scene [RIGHT] shows a ship being brought into Dutch waters in 1667, during the Four Days' Fight.

L. Backhuisen, *Boat Action on the Fourth Day of the Four Days' Fight* (detail).

Italian cartographic painting, *The Battle of Lepanto* (detail).

Lepanto, the greatest Mediterranean sea battle of the sixteenth century, was fought in the Gulf of Corinth, October 7, 1572, between the combined fleets of Spain, Venice and the Pope and that of the Ottoman Sultan. It resulted in a Christian victory and a temporary check to the extension of Moslem power over the eastern Mediterranean. This example of cartographic painting shows the Christian fleet, under the command of Don John of Austria, on the left, and Ali Monizindade's fleet penned against the coast, on the right. The battle was an inshore engagement and the tactics very largely those of land warfare.

Dec. 14th – Prisoners & deserters are continually coming in. The Army, who have been surprisingly healthy hitherto, now begin to grow very sickly from the continued fatigues they have suffered this campaign. Yet they still show spirit of alacrity & contentment not to be expected from so young troops. I am sick – discontented – and out of humor. Poor food – hard lodging – cold weather – fatigue – nasty clothes – nasty cookery – vomit half my time – smoked out of my senses – the Devil's in it – I can't endure it – why are we sent here to starve and freeze – what sweet felicities have I left at home – a charming wife – pretty children – good food – good cookery – all agreeable – all harmonious. Here, all confusion – smoke & cold – hunger & filthiness – a pox on my bad luck. Here comes a bowl of beef soup – full of burnt leaves and dirt, sickish enough to make a Hector spew – away with it Boys – I'll live like the chameleon upon air.

Surgeon Albigence Waldo in winter quarters with Washington, 1777.

William Hodges, *War Galleys at Tahiti.*

William van der Velde, the Younger, *Raid on the Dutch at Bergen*.

Johann Zoffany, *The Death of Cook*.

Hodges accompanied Captain Cook on his voyages to the South Seas, documenting the lands discovered and visited. The Tahitians were themselves voyagers to rival Cook, and their war galleys [OPPOSITE ABOVE] formidable instruments of attack, which could be driven with paddle power at high speeds over short distances.

The van der Veldes, father and son, are regarded as the greatest of all marine painters, and it is difficult to differentiate between their work. They drew their sketches of sea battles from real life, often "from a small boat in the thick of the action." This canvas [OPPOSITE BELOW] illustrates an incident in the Second Anglo-Dutch War, 1665-7, when the British admiral, Lord Sandwich, drove a Dutch convoy from the Indies into the Danish (now Norwegian) harbor of Bergen in August, 1665. He was repelled by the Danish shore batteries.

An unfinished example of the theatrical composition in which Zoffany specialized, this scene [ABOVE] shows the death of Captain Cook at Kealakekua in the Sandwich Islands, February 14, 1779, in a fracas over the theft of a ship's boat by the Polynesians.

Talking about these Zepps, reminds me of a most gruesome episode which occurred at the destruction of the first of these monsters at Cuffley, in Essex. For some months we had a man who, after being badly gassed in France, was put on to drive ambulance cars at our pier. In course of conversation one morning he told me that his car had been the first to reach the wrecked Zeppelin. Of the crew of some thirty to forty, only fourteen bodies were found on the ship, while that of the commander – only distinguishable by his uniform and medals – was discovered some few hundred yards away. It will be remembered that the ship came down in flames, and the fourteen remaining bodies were all found in a standing position grasping the steel struts of the machine with their hands. My informant told me that when they went to lift the bodies, the hands of all came off at the wrist and remained fixed on the struts! He added that the bodies were so charred that when they were laid out in a pile, previous to burial, they did not occupy the space of four normal bodies.

Stanley W. Coxon describing the destruction of the first Zeppelin over England, 1915.

Gordon Crosby, *Lieutenant Warneford's Great Exploit*.

French magazine illustration, *Gambetta Leaving Paris by Balloon*.

American engraving, *A Balloon View of the Rebel Forts and Camps at Yorktown, Virginia*.

German airship ("Zeppelin," after their constructor) attacks on England had begun in January, 1915 and, though causing little damage, provoked much alarm and anger. But the Zeppelins' great service ceiling made them difficult to destroy, and the first successful attack, on June 6, 1915, created a national sensation. This picture [OPPOSITE], which shows an LZ 32 falling in flames near Ghent on its return from a raid, is by a well-known illustrator of aviation and motor racing subjects of the period. Warneford was killed ten days after his exploit.

Léon Gambetta, Minister of the Interior in the republican government that replaced the imperial regime after its defeat at Sedan, was confined within Paris when the Prussians laid siege to the city on September 19, 1870. Determined to rally national resistance, he left the city on October 7 by one of the balloons that by then had established a regular in-and-out service from the provinces [ABOVE LEFT]. The service captured international imagination and was the first useful application of aviation to military purposes.

The employment of balloons as military observation platforms had been suggested almost as soon as the first successful ascent (1783); a Union balloon here surveys the Confederate entrenchments during the siege of Yorktown, April 4 to May 4, 1862 [ABOVE RIGHT]. Until the invention of the telephone and long-range artillery, however, the results yielded were small.

Hans Rudi Erdt, *The U-Boats Are Here*.

Planas, *An Expensive Mistake*.

This German First World War propaganda poster [OPPOSITE] brazens out the adoption of unrestricted sinking of merchant ships. It served to remind the German people that the Allied populations were also suffering from the effects of blockade.

A cartoon [LEFT] from the French war magazine, *La Baionette*, imputes to the German submarine service a breach of the law of the sea. The caption read, "A French cruiser? A thousand pardons! We took you for a neutral merchantman!" Germany had, in fact, instituted unrestricted sinkings during 1915 but suspended the policy after American protests.

Mason specialized in ship portraits; this is of an experimental "Monitor" model, which mounted a 12-inch gun [BELOW]. The class was unsuccessful. The background is of the southern tip of the Dardanelles peninsula where the British made their costly landing on April 25, 1915. The beached ship is the *River Clyde* whose embarked soldiers suffered particularly heavy losses.

Frank Mason, *H.M. Submarine M-1 off Sedd-el-Bahr*.

Kenneth Forbes, *Canadian Artillery in Action* (detail).

Forbes, a Canadian Official War Artist, has overdramatized an everyday Western Front scene of the First World War, a gun crew serving its 60-pounder [ABOVE].

Lawren P. Harris, *Tank Advance, Italy* (detail).

Paul Goranson, *Dorsal Gunner*.

A Canadian Official War Artist (and the son of a member of the Canadian "Group of Seven"), Harris shows a Sherman of the 5th Canadian Armored Division [LEFT], heavily camouflaged, in an advance up the Adriatic coastal plain during the summer of 1944.

This documentary sketch [ABOVE], perhaps for a painting, shows a gunner in the waist of a Wellington bomber belonging to a Canadian squadron based in Britain. Goranson was a Canadian Official War Artist.

Eric Kennington, *Parachutes*.

An uncharacteristically impressionistic sketch by a painter who served as a British Official War Artist in both World Wars, Kennington is best known for his illustrations to Lawrence's *Seven Pillars of Wisdom*.

Laura Knight, *Balloon Site, Coventry.*

Tethered balloons were one of the means by which the British attempted to protect their cities from German bomber attacks during the Second World War. Many of the sites were operated by women, whom Britain conscripted equally with men. Dame Laura Knight's picture was painted after the devastating attack of November 14-15, 1940, traces of which are visible in the background, and celebrates both the contribution of her sex to the war effort and the return of Coventry's factories to production.

A woman with two children joined them. "Come on," said the old man. "This looks the clearest way."

There were walls of flame round them now. Suddenly into the square came a fire engine drawn by two startled horses. They swerved aside, and one of the terrified children rushed down a side street. The mother followed, leaving her boy behind. As the first child reached a burning house some blazing wood fell near her, setting her clothes alight. The mother threw herself on top of the child to try and smother the flames, but as she did so the whole top floor of the house opposite crashed down on the two of them.

The old man grabbed the boy's hand firmly. "You come with us," he ordered.

"I'll wait for my Mummy," said the boy.

"No," said the old man, trying to make his voice sound harsh. "It's getting too hot here. We will wait for your Mummy farther away from the fire."

Elsa Windel, a survivor of the Hamburg firestorm of July 28, 1943.

This historical scene of a Second World War convoy [ABOVE] shows Hunt class destroyers and the end of an aerial attack.

Hamburg, the largest German city within easy reach of the bomber bases in Britain, was frequently and heavily attacked during the Second World War. Two British night raids, on July 26 and 29, 1943, raised a firestorm in the city, killed 40,000 inhabitants and flattened most of the buildings. This painting [RIGHT] shows British flares illuminating the target, a bomber caught in a cone of searchlights and guns on a flak tower in action.

Richard Eurich, *Destroyer Escorts Under Air Attack*.

Karl Raible, *Air Raid on Hamburg*.

An Official War Artist in both World Wars, Nash was one of the few major British painters of the period to be attracted by Surrealism. Its influence on his style is detectible in this scene of London under attack by the Luftwaffe during the Battle of Britain, 1940 [ABOVE].

Paul Nash, *Battle of Britain*.

George Horace Davis, *Closing Up*.

In mid-August, 1944, the German army in Normandy was encircled by the invading Allies, and most of its equipment destroyed, much by fighter ground attack. This picture [BELOW LEFT], by an artist who specialized in aviation pictures, is a free documentation of scenes near Falaise at the neck of the pocket. The two knocked-out German tanks in the foreground are Mark VI Panthers.

Davis was an illustrator who specialized in aviation and technical subjects; his work appeared in the *Illustrated London News* for more than thirty years. This painting [ABOVE] shows a formation of British DH-4s closing up under attack by a mixed group of German Fokker Triplanes and D-VIIs over the Western front in 1918.

Frank Wooton, *Rocket-Firing Typhoons at the Falaise Gap*.

Henry Moore, *Pink and Green Sleepers*.

The Germans air attacks on London drove many of the inhabitants of the inner city into the underground railway stations, which were designated shelters. Moore made an extensive series of sketches of the sleeping forms of the displaced in the subways [ABOVE], which are paralleled by reclining female figures in his sculptures.

The Local Defence Volunteers were called into being in June, 1940, when Britain lay open to German invasion. Sketchily uninformed and almost unarmed, they served an emotional rather than a military need. A characteristically whimsical sketch by a book-illustrator who also worked as an Official War Artist, this watercolor [RIGHT] exactly catches the rural mood of the time.

An illustration [OPPOSITE] from the magazine *The Arts* by a pupil of Whistler, its purpose was subtly propagandist at a time when America was just entering the First World War and the enthusiasm of the whole population had to be roused to the war effort.

Edward Ardizzone, *An Evening Parade of the Local Defence Volunteers in their Early Days*.

Joseph Pennell, *The Ants* from *War Work in the U.S.*

I was in it from the first. Like the volunteers of 1914, I "leapt to arms unbidden" – only there were no arms to leap to. There was nothing but an armband of white cotton crudely lettered "L.D.V." This we were instructed to dye with tea or coffee. The drilling of the L.D.V. with pikes and muskets instantly became a national joke. Actually it was propaganda to frighten the enemy, for in our company, somewhere in the Home Counties, we had not even these aids to morale. We assembled at the local drill-hall and shot off a few precious rounds of miniature ammunition; for the rest, we drilled and marched about the streets to inspire confidence. Eventually a few actual rifles were distributed – I never received one of my own, or at least not a whole one, because, although I could hit a target, I could not master the niceties of arms drill: presenting, sloping, shouldering, as taught by retired sergeants of the first World War, seemed to me useless and archaic.

James Reeves, an original
Local Defence Volunteer
(Home Guard) June 7, 1940.

V
Sieges

Unknown, *Relief of the Last Siege of Vienna*.

Organized warfare is a social activity and, though it may have its origins in the communal hunting of primitive peoples, it assumes its modern, purposive form only in comparatively advanced civilizations. The urge to take shelter from an enemy is, by contrast, a profoundly instinctual one, which man shares with many animals and expresses in similar ways, by seeking refuge on unscalable heights or in the natural openings of the rocks. Refuge and food sources by no means always coincide, however. And when they do, such coincidence may generate competition with predators or other men, which results in the expulsion of the losing party to insecure ground, where strongholds must be improvised. The cooperative employment of human manual skills may well have first been directed to such building.

Certainly excavation at the oldest city yet discovered, Jericho in the Jordan valley, reveals the existence of fortifications, now dated by carbon technique to 7000 B.C., not much younger than the earliest settlement on the site. Jericho attracted settlers because it offers both an inexhaustible supply of water and regular replenishment of the soil's fertility by silting, a rare combination of natural bounty. Once the city was established, therefore, it was to be expected that it would become an object of envy to outsiders, and that the occupants should seek to defend what they enjoyed. But what is startling about the first defenses is that they display all the features subsequently deemed essential to effective fortification by specialist engineers: continuous protection, afforded by an encompassing wall; defense in depth, provided by a secondary wall; dominance of the attacker, offered from a tall tower; and protection against undermining, secured by a moat. Since the interior allowed room for only some two thousand inhabitants, but the construction must have entailed tens of thousands of workdays, we may presume the existence of a large dependent population subsisting beyond the walls, behind which it took refuge only when danger threatened.

The fort as temporary refuge is found all over the inhabited world, often on high ground above cultivated or grazing land, notably as the acropolis ("high city") of the Mediterranean and the hill fort of Iron Age Britain. The medieval peel towers and fortified churches of

A contemporary narrative painting, this scene depicts the arrival of John Sobieski of Poland at the head of the relief army on September 12, 1683. In a few hours' fighting the Polish forces dispersed the great Turkish army, which had laid siege to Vienna since July 17. Sobieski is portrayed as a Christian conqueror, and his victory was indeed hailed throughout Christendom as an almost miraculous deliverance. The campaign was the last in which the Ottomans attempted an invasion of Western Europe.

the Scottish borders are a survival of the type. But most forts probably always offered a permanent residence to the ruler and his specialized fighting men and, as the settled populations they protected enriched themselves by trade or war or a combination of the two, grew in size to enclose the dwellings of all non-agricultural dependants. The defeat of an enemy so accommodated, if he had sufficient food stored to outlast an invasion of his outlying territory, required a direct attack on his position. And as prosperity also permitted the deliberate siting of cities to exploit geographical advantage — usually control of a river, natural highway or sea defile or harbor — such attacks would come to have the force of strategic necessity to a threatened or competitive neighbor. Hence the development of the special art of siege warfare.

A successful siege employs one or more of five methods: breaching, when a portion of the wall is destroyed by the application of direct fire to its face; mining, when it is caused to subside; escalade, when it is overtopped by an assault party (or by their missiles, which may be combustible, pestiferous or toxic); and ruse or treachery, which secures the opening of the gates from within. If all fails, starvation, assisted by the onset of disease, is the besieger's last weapon. But since starvation and disease are fates to which besieging armies themselves are notably prone, direct attack has strong attractions, not only for the impatient aggressor. It was certainly attempted from the earliest times — the nature of Jericho's defenses is evidence of that — and was brought to a high level of refinement by the Assyrians. Their siege trains included battering rams and moveable towers, from which missiles were shot into the interior of the city. The methods were not infallible; Sennacherib failed before the walls of Jerusalem in 701 B.C., perhaps because disease broke out in his lines. But their employment was generally successful enough to extend the boundaries of the Assyrian empire from the Caucasus to Egypt in the eighth century B.C.

Ruse was a favored siege method of the Greeks in antiquity. Employed at Troy, it brought to an end the most famous siege in history — for if the *Iliad* is a collection of myths, the events it describes are rooted in fact. But the most important Greek contribution to the technique of siege warfare was the invention of the catapult, apparently first seen at Syracuse at the end of the fifth century B.C. There it was used to defend the walls, which were furnished with high towers at regular intervals to provide the weapon with firing platforms. Means were soon found, however, to make it mobile, and it became the most important element in

Alexander's siege train, with which he reduced a succession of fortresses on his march of conquest from Macedon to India. In the hands of Roman engineers, it multiplied in form to fire heavy arrows and bolts in flat trajectories as well as boulders in ballistic ones. All were frequently employed, for the spread of Rome's power stemmed as much from her ability to reduce the fortified cities of her enemies as to defeat their armies in pitched battle. The first great crisis of Roman expansion, the war against Carthage, was ultimately resolved by the siege and destruction of that city. And the conquest of Gaul was consolidated only by the investment and capture of the fortresses on which the Gauls centered the rebellion they had raised against Roman occupation.

Last and greatest of the Gallic sieges was at Alesia, near the source of the Seine, in 52 B.C. Caesar, though outnumbered, succeeded in confining Vercingetorix within the walls, which he surrounded with a double barrier of his own, the first to protect his army against sallies by the defenders, the second against attack by a relieving force. Known as lines of circumvallation and contravallation, they would be revived as a standard feature of investment in the great age of siege warfare seventeen hundred years later. And their worth was proved on the spot, for Vercingetorix's confederates appeared in overwhelming numbers during the course of operations and were held at bay chiefly by this means.

The subsequent extension and internal pacification of the Roman world in the first and second centuries A.D. ended such disturbing events. And in the process it revolutionized urban architecture. For, probably for the first time in human history, towns were now built without walls, because citizens could place their trust in the security of distant frontiers. It was imperial policy, indeed, to deny fortification to towns, lest they fell into the hands of invaders or rebels. The two-year siege of the Jewish Zealots at Masada (72-73 A.D.) was a reminder, if the emperors needed one, of how tiresome insurgents with access to a stronghold could be. But the lapse of fortification in the imperial interior did not mean its disappearance from the Roman military system. On the contrary, during the second and third centuries, the Empire embarked on the construction of the largest system of fortification known in the western world. In the Far East, a region of which Romans had heard only by fragmentary travelers' tales, the Chinese emperors had already erected their enormous Great Wall to exclude the barbarians of Inner Asia. Now known to have been four thousand miles long at its greatest extent, it far outstripped the works of the Romans as an engineering achievement.

But theirs was impressive enough. On the African and Near Eastern frontiers, they constructed a chain of mutually supporting forts connected by a frontier road; on the Rhine and Danube a barrier of ramparts and ditches (the *Limes*); and across the neck of northern Britain a continuous wall, the relics of which, even today, bear comparison with that of China.

Continuous frontier fortification is the hallmark of rich, stable states and was to return with their re-emergence in the sixteenth century. But frontiers, however strongly fortified, are not self-defending. For security they require the presence of an effective army in their rear. However, for economic but perhaps also for psychological reasons, armies and fortifications, representing the principles of active and passive defense, tend to be antithetical. It is significant that the cities of the most aggressive of all military peoples, the Mongols, were surrounded by purely symbolic walls. And Rome's institution of fixed fortifications on her borders was indeed shortly succeeded by the decline of her army and the re-walling of towns within the frontier zone, evidence of the army's inability to prevent the incursion in depth of barbarians from outside. Their wholesale irruption in the fifth century destroyed both army and frontier. And the resulting disorder, where it did not altogether extinguish urban life, prompted the refortification of cities all over western Europe and the building of new strongholds to shelter the war bands of local men of power.

The history of the rise of modern states is very much that of the reduction of these personal castles (all the more necessary when held by mere robber barons) and of the building of others by rising royal houses to protect the frontiers of their authority. The crusader castles guarding the borders of the Latin Kingdoms in the Holy Land provide the best known example of a systematic castle chain. Edward I's girdle of castles along and within the border of Wales and the Emperor Frederick II's complex of strongholds in southern Italy are others. Geography dictated individual choice of site; the intervals between were calculated by the radius of action of the mounted garrison a castle contained, so that neighbors could assist each other in time of trouble. So strong were European late-medieval castles relative to contemporary means of attack, however, that garrisons were usually able to survive all but the longest siege, which only rich rulers were able to mount. That of Richard the Lionheart's Château-Gaillard by Philip II of France lasted from 1203-4 and was concluded only by the most laborious undermining of its concentric lines of defense.

Too often, moreover, at times of rebellion or state penury, royal castles reverted to private hands, and the work had to be done again, as in England during the Wars of the Roses and France during the Hundred Years' War. Not until the appearance of efficient cannon in the fifteenth century did the balance tip decisively against the private castellan and in favor of central authority. For cannon were too expensive for private buyers and too powerful for traditional fortifications to withstand. Indeed the very principle which the castle exemplified, height above the head of an attacker, rendered it particularly vulnerable to artillery attack. Cannonade against the base quickly enlisted the aid of gravity to bring the whole mass tumbling down, usually to fill the ditch or moat and so provide a handy bridge into the interior. In 1494, Charles VIII of France invaded Italy with a siege train of forty of the new guns and took all the castles on his route from Leghorn to Naples in a few months. The castle of Monte San Giovanni, which had once withstood siege by the old methods for seven years, was breached in eight hours.

Gunpowder was not, however, a European invention, and the use of cannon never a European monopoly. The Ottoman Turks were early and skillful artillerists and it was their great guns which at last crowned with success their two centuries of struggle to overthrow Byzantium at the final siege of Constantinople in 1453. That victory threatened the whole of Christian Europe north of the Balkans and the Turks would indeed carry siege to Vienna in 1529. Miraculously its medieval walls withstood the Turks' assault, and when they returned in 1683 the fortifications had been remodeled on a new system which nullified their cannon's power. Developed in Italy in the sixteenth century, it reversed the old principles, substituting depth for height, to the point where its elaborate geometrical pattern of bastion and ravelin was scarcely visible above the surface. This "bastion trace" had already defeated another Turkish line of advance on Malta in 1565. Applied to the defenses of northern Italy, the Pyrenees and above all the Low Countries, where bastion fortresses were constructed against each other by the French, Dutch and Habsburgs on every river crossing place of importance, it was to make the free movement of armies almost impossible during the late seventeenth and much of the eighteenth century.

In the world outside Europe, where old methods prevailed, as in India and Japan, castles would continue to tremble to cannon wherever they made their appearance. They were a principal ingredient in the Moguls' conquest of India and also naturally of the Conquistadores' destruction of the Aztec and Inca strongholds in the

Americas. And fortifications in the European colonies, often sketchily built because money was locally scarce, would yield to determined or ingenious attack, as at Quebec which Wolfe took by amphibious assault in 1759. But it was not until the appearance of mass armies, large enough to swamp whole defended belts, as in the wars of the French Revolution, that freedom to manoeuvre was restored to campaigning generals in Europe. The victories of Napoleon, though he was a gunner who had first made his name at the siege of Toulon in 1793, seemed to render fortification irrelevant and certainly devalued its worth in the professional mind, which was concentrated for much of the nineteenth century on efforts to systematize methods of fighting in the open field.

Yet much money continued to be spent, paradoxically, on forts which, as artillery grew in power and mobility, became even more elaborate than in the great era of siege warfare two hundred years earlier. The defenses of Paris in 1870 were extensive and powerful enough to withstand a Prussian siege of five months, and they continued to be improved until 1914. But it was the improvement of small arms rather than heavy guns which eventually restored real importance to fixed defenses. Infantry firepower, enormously increased by the breech-loading rifle and then by the machine gun, first obliged armies to improvise extensive field entrenchments during the American Civil War. By the beginning of the twentieth century, such entrenchments might cover a whole front of operations, as in Manchuria during the Russo-Japanese War of 1904-5. And, to the surprise of all combatants, both the eastern and western fronts in the First World War, respectively five and seven hundred miles long, were entrenched in their entirety almost immediately after its outbreak.

Many attempts have been made to explain the strange and terrible nature of the fighting between 1914-18. It is undoubtedly best understood if thought of as a mutual siege on a gigantic scale. Not only is that true because of both sides' early recourse to the strategy of starvation through blockade. Blockade has always been a means which besiegers seek to apply, both by land and more particularly by sea. Instituted with stringency by the Allies in 1914, it progressively deprived the Central Powers of essential war materials. And when Germany responded with a submarine blockade of Britain, it brought that island within sight of starvation during 1917.

Germany was finally defeated not by blockade but by the Allies' discovery of a means to crack their fortifications on the Western Front: the tank. In its original form, it can be seen as a revival of the battering ram and siege tower. In the Second World War, in a developed form, it restored such mobility to the operations of armies in the field that fixed fronts were much less frequent in the fighting, and those which had been constructed at leisure, like the Maginot Line in France and the Mareth Line in North Africa, were nullified by rapid advances elsewhere. The practice of blockade was re-instituted with even more severity than in the First World War, however, and to its effect was added that of direct missile attack on the population within the defended fronts. The power and range of the bombing aircraft transformed the whole territory of combatant states into fortress interiors, within which security could be assured to the population only by providing them with air raid shelters. The protection of the war industries which fed the fighting could scarcely be assured at all. This transformation, which made every inhabitant willy-nilly a warrior, demanded of all a personal commit-ment to victory never previously expected of civilians. Their resili-ence in every country which experienced aerial bombardment was one of the war's few heartening manifestations, sustaining belief in the durability of the human spirit and its power to survive even the worst that siege can bring.

On another side, our knights fought the enemy daily, erecting ladders against the walls of the town. But the pagans resisted so strongly that our men could make no progress. Meanwhile, Goufier of Lastours was the first to reach the top of the wall by a ladder; but immediately the ladder broke under the weight of his too numerous companions. However, he and a few others managed to get on to the wall. Others, having found another ladder, quickly propped it against the wall. But the Saracens attacked them with such force, both on the wall and on the ground, shooting their arrows and pointing their lances at them at close range, that many of our men, struck with terror, threw themselves from the top of the wall.

While those valiant men who remained on the crest of the wall were enduring these attacks, those who were below the castle were sapping the walls of the town. When the Saracens saw that we had sapped their wall, they were seized with terror and fled into the city. All this took place on Saturday, December 11th, at sunset, the hour of vespers.

Siege of Jerusalem by the Crusaders,
First Crusade, 1099.

Moghul manuscript illumination,
Akbar Besieges Ranthambor.

Flemish manuscript illumination, *Siege of Jerusalem by Saladin*.

This illustration [OPPOSITE], an excellent example of Moghul work, is of an episode of Akbar conquest of Rajputana in 1569-70. The Rajputs were the most warlike of Akbar's Hindu enemies but were eventually forced to submit to his power. Ranthambor is a typical Hindu hill fortress of great strength; the guns on the right are firing at the defenders rather than the walls. The site made the emplacement of siege batteries impossible.

Saladin's defeat of the Crusader army at Hattin on July 4, 1187 allowed him to mount a general offensive against the Latin Kingdom of Jerusalem, and on October 2 he succeeded in recapturing the Holy City after a two-week siege. This illustration [ABOVE] from de Bouillon's *Hercules' Conquest of Jerusalem*, represents in a stylized form the technique of mid-fifteenth-century siege warfare in Western Europe.

Jean Fouquet, *Battle Scene*.

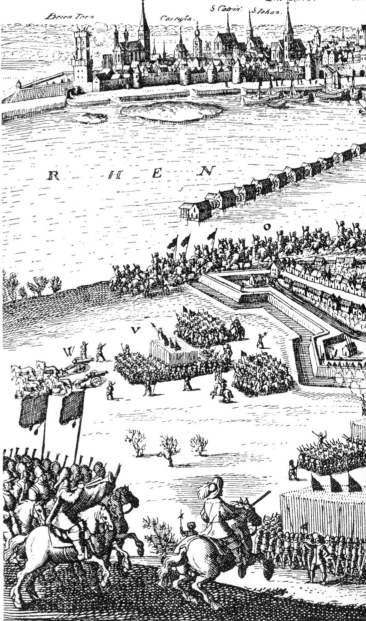

This illumination [ABOVE] is of a skirmish before a castle, from which one of the parties has perhaps just made a sortie.

This "analytical" engraving [RIGHT] of a siege of the Thirty Years' War shows Gustavus Adolphus's attack on Cologne during his Rhineland offensive of 1632. In the background stands the old city behind its medieval walls; in the foreground, the new suburb of Deutz, defended by modern bastion fortification. A powder magazine in the church has exploded and the Swedish infantry have succeeded in forcing an entrance by one of the northern gates.

German engraving, *Swedish Attack on Deutz and Cologne.*

French manuscript illustration, *Battle of Damietta*.

When the army of the Christians arrived before Damietta in the land of Egypt, fearless Brother Francis, armed with the buckler of the faith...advanced towards the Sultan of Egypt. When the Saracens seized him on his way, he said: "I am a Christian, lead me to your master." When they had brought him there, the fierce beast, on seeing him, was turned to gentleness by the aspect of the man of God and listened very attentively to the sermon on Christ which he preached for several days to him and the people.

Cardinal James of Vitry describes Saint Francis of Assisi's visit to the Sultan of Egypt at the Siege of Damietta, 1219.

In the middle of the twelfth century the Crusaders attempted to extend their power from Palestine into Egypt. For two years, 1167-9, they held Cairo but were eventually driven out by a Moslem success at Damietta. This illustration [OPPOSITE] comes from the *Histoire du voyage et conquete de Jerusalem*, 1337.

A flight of whimsy by the illuminator, this picture [BELOW] illustrates some of the techniques and impedimenta of medieval siege warfare. The donkey is working a trebuchet or mangonel, which threw projectiles into a fortress by counter-weight.

Dutch manuscript illumination, *Foxes Besieging a Fortress*.

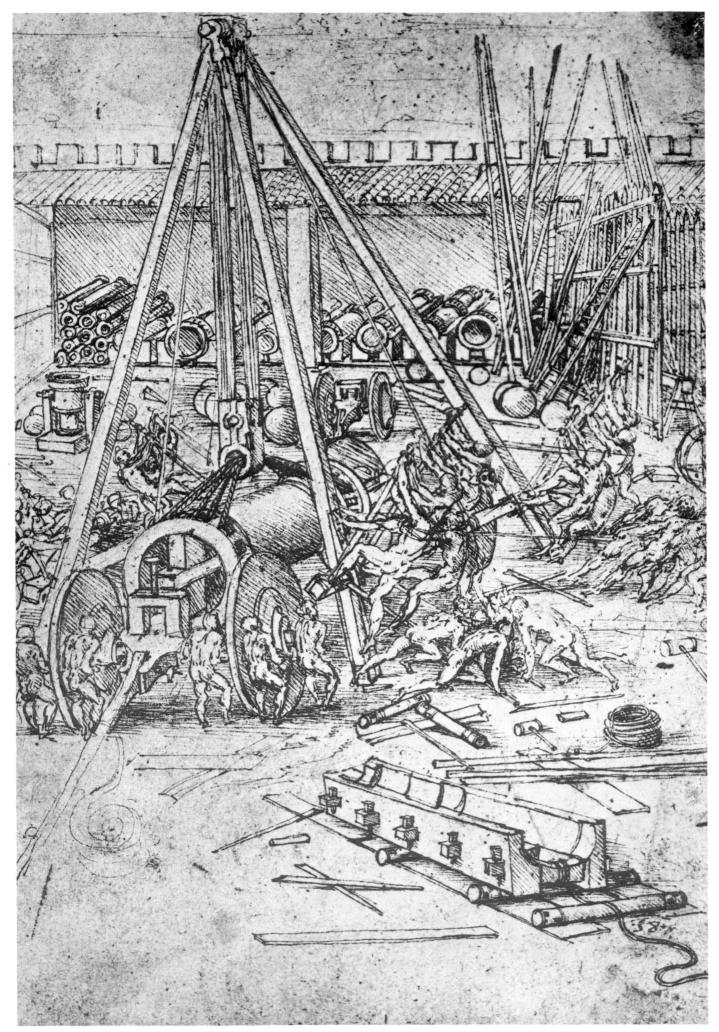

Leonardo da Vinci, *Mounting a Cannon on its Carriage*.

Edward Poynter, *The Catapult* (detail).

This drawing [OPPOSITE] is more likely a work of Leonardo's imagination than a sketch from life. The cannon, of the two-part variety which unscrewed for loading, is bigger even than any of the monsters fashionable in the period. It is being swung up on sheer legs for mounting on its traveling wheels; its firing platform lies in the foreground.

Poynter was an immensely successful painter of the historical pictures, so beloved by rich Victorians, of exact archeological detail and romantic composition. This scene [ABOVE] purports to be of the Roman siege of Carthage, which ended the Punic Wars in 146 B.C. The soldiers are working a ballista, which threw projectiles by force of torsion. The artist was a brother-in-law to Rudyard Kipling, and his images may have helped feed that writer's powerful historical imagination.

Japanese screen painting, *The Siege of Osaka* (detail).

A scene from the civil war of 1614-15. Opponents of the newly founded Tokugawa Shogunate (hereditary ministry) raised the standard of revolt at Osaka castle. The Tokugawa forces besieged it from December, 1614 to June, 1615, when they succeeded in carrying it by storm after having filled in part of the moat during a truce.

Italian cartographic painting, *The Siege of Malta*.

The Turkish siege of the fortress of the Knights of St. John on Malta in 1565 was one of the crucial military events of the sixteenth century in Southern Europe. The knights sustained resistance for five months, in conditions of terrible hardship, until relieved by a Spanish fleet; their tenacity put a check to the hitherto apparently irresistible westward spread of Ottoman power in the Mediterranean. This magnificent map shows the Turkish encampments and anchorages, the Fort of St. Elmo, top center, the focus of the siege, and the new fortified city of Valetta, right, which held out after St. Elmo had fallen.

Lienzo de Maxcala,
The Attack on the Great Temple.

Hermando Cortés' reckless invasion of the Aztec empire in 1518, with a force of only six hundred men, culminated in his successful siege of the capital of Tenochtilán, May to August, 1521. This picture [ABOVE] by a Mexican artist shows the final assault on the Great Temple, in which the emperor, Cuauhtemoc, was captured. The assault party is composed of Spaniards and their Mexican allies; the artist has taken special care with the depiction of the Spaniards' armor and horses, which, with their ferocious self-confidence, gave the conquerors their military superiority.

The Anglo-French struggle for mastery in North America culminated in 1759 in a four-month siege of the main French stronghold at Quebec on the St. Lawerence river [OPPOSITE]. Apparently impregnable, it was eventually taken when General James Wolfe was shown a way up the cliffs to its rear. His amphibious assault forced the French to fight in the open on the Plains of Abraham in September. He was killed at the moment of victory.

English engraving, *A View of the Taking of Quebec* (detail).

Yesterday afternoon a pigeon arrived covered with blood, bearing on its tail a dispatch from Gambetta, of the 11th, announcing that the Prussians had been driven out of Orleans after two days' fighting, that 1,000 prisoners, two cannon, and many munition waggons had been taken, and that the pursuit was still continuing. The dispatch was read at the Mairies to large crowds, and in the cafés by enthusiasts, who got upon the tables. I was in a shop when a person came in with it. Shopkeeper, assistants and customers immediately performed a war dance round a stove; one would have supposed that the war was over and that the veracity of Gambetta is unimpeachable. But as though this success were not enough in itself, all the newspapers this morning tell us that Chartres has also been retaken, that the army of Kératry has effected a junction with that of the Loire, and that in the north Bourbaki has forced the Prussians to raise the siege of Amiens. Edmond About, in the *Soir*, eats dirt for having a few days ago suggested an armistice.

A resident describes an incident during the Siege of Paris, November 15, 1870.

Ernest Meissonier, *Allegory of the Siege of Paris*.

Meissonier's composition [LEFT] groups representatives of the various elements of the Paris garrison that resisted the Prussian siege of September, 1870 to January, 1871 around a sombre goddess of victory. Regular soldiers are in the foreground, naval artillerymen to the left, civilian *gardes mobiles* to the right. The most accomplished of the French nineteenth-century nationalist historical painters, Meissonier served at the front during the war.

Detaille was at his best in documentary reportage. Here he shows the improvisation of a barricade in a southern suburb of Paris on the day the Prussians laid siege to the city [BELOW]. The figures include infantrymen, gunners, sappers and some cavalry spectators.

Edouard Detaille, *Episode in the Siege of Paris, Villejuif, September 19, 1870*.

Meissonier's most famous Napoleonic painting [RIGHT] shows the Emperor riding with his generals in the final campaign before Waterloo.

Painted in a typical propagandist style, this shows a struggle in a Second World War town [BELOW].

Ernest Meissonier, *1814*.

V. Pamfilov, *Exploits of the Panfilov Guards*.

Unknown, *Indians Besiege Spaniards in Tenochtitlán*.

Cortés, who had been allowed to enter the Aztec capital as a guest on November 8, 1519, subsequently provoked Montezuma's subjects to violence by his high-handedness and double-dealing. On June 30, 1520, the Spaniards were driven out of the city. The emperor, whom Cortés had seized, can be seen [ABOVE] next to the priest among the armored warriors. He was killed by the Spaniards during the fighting.

Parma, captured by Francis I of France in 1515, was chosen by Pope Leo X as the focus of his counter-offensive in 1519. The attack was led by his Medici kinsman, Giovanni delle Banda Nere, so-called because of the color of the armor worn by his private army (one of its pikemen stands in the foreground of Tintoretto's picture [OPPOSITE]). Giovanni successfully led the assault party, seen scaling the walls in the background.

Jacobo Tintoretto, *Capture of Parma* (detail).

Robert Bonnard after Pieter Vandermeulen and C. leBrun, *Siege of Tournai* (detail).

Pieter Vandermeulen, *Louis XIV's Army Resting in Front of Tournai*.

In the short Franco-Spanish War of Devolution, 1667-8, Louis XIV invaded the Spanish Netherlands to enforce a claim on the throne of Spain. Tournai, a much-besieged frontier town, was quickly taken. This excellent documentary [OPPOSITE ABOVE], a cartoon for a tapestry, shows musketeers and pikemen moving up the approach trenches to assault the walls, which are under fire from siege artillery. In the foreground lie brushwood bundles used for entrenchment.

This engraving after a painting by Louis XIV's battle painter [OPPOSITE BELOW] shows the French army in camp before the wall of Tournai; seventeenth-century armies on campaign were encumbered with large numbers of civilians, who fed the soldiers and drove the animals.

Sixteenth- and seventeenth-century Dutch art is rich in examples of anti-war themes, in which the cruelties of the Spanish or (as here) the French are portrayed with a vigor that may not be exaggerated [LEFT].

Romijl del Hooghe, *Louis XIV's War in the Netherlands*.

Otto Dix, *Self-Portrait as a Prisoner*.

Dix, a member of the German "New Objectivity" group, made his reputation with his anti-war paintings after the First World War. During the Nazi regime he was arrested by the Gestapo as a "decadent" painter. This self-portrait [OPPOSITE] partakes of both his military and political experiences.

Brest-Litovsk was one of the fortified towns overrun by the Germans during the first months of their invasion of Russia in 1941. This painting [RIGHT], which emphasizes the unity of soldiers and civilians, men and women, in resisting the invader, typifies the character of Soviet patriotic art.

Byelorussian painter, *Defenders of the Fortress of Brest-Litovsk*.

My pass was from midday on Saturday, and I got down to the centre of London by Underground. Bombers were coming over at monotonously regular intervals. I walked down to Charing Cross. There was a lot of noise still, and a lot of smoke. As I entered the station the loudspeakers were ordering everyone out because planes were overhead and they were frightened of casualties if the place were hit. I strolled out to the top of that long flight of stone steps down into Villiers Street and sat on the balustrade watching.

Up in the lonely sky there was still one bomber, gleaming silver, and then he dropped a stick just across the Thames from us. Back in the station the loudspeaker announced that the main line was gone and that there wouldn't be any more trains out for hours.

Private Desmond Flower in London during the Battle of Britain, August, 1940.

A watercolor of London during the Blitz, by an Official War Artist and leading English portrait painter. "Britain Can Take It" was one of the slogans propagated by the Ministry of Information during 1940-1 while Britain was under German air attack.

Ruskin Spear, *We Can Take It*.

VI
Battles

Albrecht Altdorfer, *The Battle of Issus*.

*"Tweedledum and Tweedledee
Agreed to have a battle."*

Well brought up Victorian children were taught to laugh at the joke. But, like so many of Lewis Carroll's, it hints at a profound truth. Much that goes on in warfare — ambush, surprise, attack, siege, blockade — is wished by one party on the other, who must respond as best he can. Guerrilla warfare, which has become a staple form of conflict in the late twentieth century, is indeed the institutionalization of unwanted combat by a weaker party on a stronger, and all the more resented by reason of that disparity; hence its equation with treachery and even crime, to the methods of which the guerrilla fighter often resorts. Battle partakes of a different moral atmosphere. It may be inflicted on an unwilling party by a skillful general who has outmanoeuvred his opponent in space or time, by backing the enemy's army against an impassable obstacle or exhausting his efforts at evasion or delay. It may be made the unavoidable outcome of a campaign in which one side masses greater numbers against the other, either by their possession from the outset or by stratagems which cause the ill judged diversion of portions of the enemy force from the main theater of operations. But, though the beaten party may subsequently repine, he will rarely enjoy the world's sympathy. For, despite all its unspeakable horrors, the battlefield is recognized as a Court of Justice, rough justice without doubt, but one in which neither side is compelled, unless by unwisdom or perversity, to fight the issue through to a verdict, as long, that is, as surrender is an option which the enemy will entertain. And entertain it, while the supplicant retains his weapons and cohesion, reason usually impels him to do. An encounter, however contrived, which results in combat may therefore be regarded as having an outcome to which both parties have given their consent.

Such agreement presupposes a match and mutual understanding of weapons and methods. What we can still see of battles between primitive peoples confirms that this is so. In New Guinea, battle is so

Issus (333 B.C.) was the first battle between the Persian Emperor Darius and Alexander during the conqueror's advance into the Middle East. Altdorfer, who painted this for a series of battle pieces of antiquity commissioned by the Duke of Bavaria, has represented the engagement in the military style of his own time: tents, standards, armor and weapons are exactly portrayed; only the size of the armies and the density of their formations are exaggerated. The angle of vision is, of course, entirely artistic and helps make this one of the greatest of all battle pieces.

carefully staged that death is rarely inflicted, not from any taboo against killing, which is common in random inter-village raiding, but because of a lively appreciation of how fatal *real* battle could be; a careful mutual keeping of distance just outside known missile range is maintained. Some anthropologists have accordingly characterized such affairs as mere rituals. But it seems, on the contrary, that they do perform an important function in tribal relations, and that what restrains the participants from real heroics is lack of motive. The tribes are noted for a strong sense of place, their ethos is weak in concepts of authority and population density is low. Hence, enemies lack both the idea of and drive toward territorial conquest.

Battle was purposively transformed when the need or desire to take and hold a neighbor's land first laid hold of a warrior society. When that may have been we can only guess, but inter-city battles were an established feature of Greek life in the seventh century B.C. Earnest and bloody though they were, they were not, however, annihilatory because both sides too closely resembled each other in armament and tactics for one to win a decisive advantage over the other. Such advantage, stemming usually from clear technological superiority, must nevertheless have already been achieved else-where, for archeological evidence of very rapid cultural change at Mesopotamian sites suggests wholesale conquest of one people by another two or three thousand years earlier. It is best explained by the defeat of inferior by superior weapons. That explanation becomes even more convincing if it is accepted that a move to a higher technology also entails a refinement of social organization through the heightening of specialization. The management of a society of specialists requires the imposition of authority and acquiescence to it, and that ethos readily translates into the urge to extend authority over others. When authority, technical superiority and the territorial urge combine, the stage is set for conquest through battle.

We may verify this supposition by reference to the battle between the Pharaoh Tuthmosis III and the King of Kadesh at Megiddo in Palestine in 1469 B.C., the first in history of which we have a detailed account. The Pharaoh's enemies were rebels attempt-ing to regain their independence. The threat they offered was therefore a dual one, to his authority and to the territorial integrity of his empire. After careful reconnaissance of their chosen position, an imposing one in the Plain of Esdraeleon, supported by the high stronghold of Megiddo, Tuthmosis advanced in a concave formation, outflanked the rebels on the right and so enveloped and destroyed their army. Victory thus derived from his organizational superiority. A similar superiority underlay the success of that other great Middle Eastern empire, the Assyrian, which learned to combine in its army the different effects of spearmen, archers, charioteers and massed cavalry into an irresistible battlefield force. But the supreme exemplification of imperial military power in the ancient world was, of course, the Roman army. Indeed, the particular distinction of the Legions of the Empire was that, though equipped with weapons not at all superior to those of their enemies, they were nevertheless almost always and everywhere triumphant. Their secret lay in the relentless consistency with which they performed their battlefield drills in the face of the enemy who, whatever he may have thought he had agreed to when giving battle, was very rarely able to match the iron discipline of that long-service army. With its disappearance in the fifth century, victory or defeat on western battlefields once again became haphazard, chiefly determined by the relative ferocity of the barbarian hosts which replaced it or by the short-lived cohesion which a more than usually determined leader managed to impose on his new band.

About the eighth century, however, important technical innovations entered the European style of making war, which would return the power of decision to those who mastered their implications. The most important one was the introduction of the stirrup. Simple though it is, it invests the rider with vastly improved control over his mount, allowing him to charge in armor against the enemy, bearing a lance which the horse's speed endows with great shock force. Hitherto cavalry had never played more than an ancillary role in warfare; thereafter it became for eight hundred years the dominant arm, to be opposed only by infantry either foolhardy — like Harold's axemen at Hastings — or with a remarkable mastery of their weapons and belief in each other. The English archers at Agincourt possessed that mastery over a weapon which local art had brought to the highest possible level of its development.

But Agincourt was an isolated check to the unbroken run of cavalry superiority which was to be ended only by a genuine technological revolution ushered in by gunpowder. Its influence was slow to make itself felt. Primitive cannon appeared on the battlefield as early as the fourteenth century; Edward III of England had some at Crécy in 1346. But, though developed by the end of the fifteenth century to the point where they nullified the value of traditional fortifications, it would be another century before reliable small arms would break the tactical dominance of the horseman, and another two after that until artillery would be made mobile enough to take its place on the battlefield.

The appearance of these new weapons nevertheless demanded a new sort of army, because their expense exceeded the means of the private feudal warrior and required for a proper return on the supplier's outlay a longer term of service in the field than he, with his part-time obligation, would provide. Mercenaries — professionals serving for pay — had already made their appearance in late-medieval armies, as in that of Florence, whose defeat of the Sienese at San Romano in 1432 suggested the subject for the most famous of all battle pictures. Those who offered firearms in their contract were now eagerly hired by the northern Italian cities, newly rich on the profits of revived Mediterranean trade, and by the rising monarchies, which were learning to tax their subjects regularly and efficiently. With their help, the surviving feudal arrays and the older mercenary contingents which clung to edged weapons, like the Swiss who met the French at Marignano in 1515, were easily trounced. When mercenaries, whose bought loyalty was always dubious, began to be replaced by permanently enlisted regulars, as by the Spanish, the "military revolution" of the sixteenth century would be complete. The Spanish victory over the French at Pavia in 1525 demonstrated its decisive nature. And the appearance in Germany at the beginning of the seventeenth century of armies, like that of Gustavus Adolphus of Sweden, which were not only regular but recruited exclusively on the national territory, completed its effect.

Regular pay and supply, national recruitment and the management of firearms by carefully regulated and endlessly practiced drills were the ingredients which would determine the character of battle for the next two hundred years. But armies so organized and equipped, like those of Marlborough and Louis XIV, found it difficult, when well matched, to secure any advantage over each other, except at the cost of terrible casualties, incurred in firepower duels at short range which black powder imposed. Frederick the Great learned something of the art of securing a decision by imbuing his army with the ability to manoeuvre rapidly on the battlefield. To the same art, Napoleon added that of the massing of artillery, the effect of which he exploited with the great reserves of cavalry he added to his Grand Army. Against an inferior enemy, like the Spanish whom he met at Somo Sierra in 1808, the effect of those combined elements could be devastating; opposed by a general like Wellington who would agree to fight only where the ground suited the defense, as at Waterloo, his methods could misfire disastrously.

The four hundred years of gunpowder warfare in Europe, culminating perhaps in the Crimean battles like the Alma, were indeed to see stalemate more often than decision. Beyond its bounds, where Europeans, or their imitators like the Japanese, brought superior technology to bear against primitive weapons, the trend was, of course, entirely contrary. Even so, as Custer found at the Little Big Horn and the British at Isandhlwana, the fighting spirit of warrior peoples might still on occasion overcome the firepower of Europeans overconfident of their superiority. But the second military-technological revolution, exemplified by the breech-loading rifle and the machine gun ("Whatever happens/We have got/ The Maxim gun/And they have not" — Hilaire Belloc), transferred battlefield power decisively to the industrial nations. Its character was first glimpsed in the battles of the American Civil War, as at Gettysburg where intemperate attacks broke under the lash of the defenders' rapid-firing weapons, incurring casualties so numerous that the decision passed by default to the other side. Those who persisted in trying to make the old methods work, as both French and Prussians tried in 1870, suffered painful casualties as a result. And by the end of the nineteenth century, after a short-lived period of fluidity in battlefield events, industrial weapon power would drive both attacker and defender to seek protection from its effects in entrenchments. During the Russo-Japanese War of 1904-5, operations indeed culminated in the entrenchment of fronts over extended areas. In the First World War, all fronts in France, Russia and in the Turkish theaters were rapidly entrenched across their entire lengths.

At sea, the impact of industrialization had had a contrary effect, liberating navies from the constrictions which had so often led to statemate in the gunpowder era. Before its onset, naval battle had been little different from land battle in character, the ships providing platforms from which their crews might fight each other with sword and mace when ranges were closed to boarding distance; Lepanto exemplified such events on the largest scale. The embarkation of the "great gun" had ushered in a period when true victories could be won at sea, but it had been brief. The defeat of the Spanish Armada owed as much to the weather as to English gunnery, and when all navies came to be equipped with similar artillery batteries, most sea fights — like the Anglo-Dutch engagement at the Texel — took on the character of stand-offs. Trafalgar, a brilliant exception to the norm, was the outcome of the application of a mind of genius, Nelson's, to the solution of the difficulties which obliged the attacker to desist whenever the defender chose to break off an engagement.

Those difficulties stemmed ultimately from dependence on the wind which always allowed the defender to make his escape when battle grew too hot. Steam power conferred a manoeuvrability which an aggressive admiral could use to negate that option. When supplemented with the power of the heavy breech-loading gun, it transformed the battleship into an instrument of decisive offensive action. In the first duel between ironclad steamships, the *Merrimac-Monitor* fight in the American Civil War, neither vessel was a sufficiently developed example of the type to drive advantage home. But the central encounter of the Russo-Japanese war at sea, Tsushima, culminated in the total destruction of the Russian fleet. The naval battles of the First World War, at Coronel, the Falkland Islands, the Dogger Bank and Jutland, ended either in the same way or with crippling loss of material to one side or the other. And the sea battles of the Second World War, in which the airplane operating from a specialized carrier proved the decisive arm, were as frequently total in their outcome as anything achieved by mechanized military power on land.

There, the stalemates of 1914-18 had driven generals, particularly in defeated Germany, to seek new means of overcoming the weight of firepower which industrialization had put into the hands of the defense. The most promising was the tank, with which in 1940 and 1941 the German armies won victories in France and Russia as spectacular in their quickness and totality as any achieved by those earlier masters of mobility, the Mongol horsemen of Central Asia. So threatening was Germany's success, however, that it evoked a response from her enemies even more terrible than the attacks visited on them. On land the Allies, eastern and western, soon outbuilt Germany in tanks and forced her to fight battles of attrition, the cost of which counted as much in human as in material terms, exceeded her resources to pay. In the air the bombing airplane, whose silhouette had menaced civilians ever since the raid on Guernica in 1937, brought devastation directly into the German homeland, where the Luftwaffe's fighters were defeated in their own sky by the intruders' long-range escorts. And at sea, though Germany's chief weapon, the submarine, at first fought the Allies' surface fleet on advantageous terms, new weapons and methods eventually carried the advantage decisively to the Allied side. Most dramatic of these developments was that of the fully amphibious landing force. In the Pacific, combined fleets of warships and beaching craft, protected by great aerial flotillas, robbed the Japanese of one island stronghold after another. In the Mediterranean and the English

Channel, the Allied navies debarked whole armies, which brought their own artillery and tanks directly onto the beaches from shipboard and engaged the enemy in conventional battle from the water's edge.

So overwhelming had the industrial nations' battle-fighting capacity become by 1945 that those who sought to oppose them, particularly their colonial subject peoples in Asia and Africa, rightly seized on the perception that agreement to fight on their terms was self-defeating. Mao Tse-tung in China, Ho Chi Minh in Vietnam, Boumedienne in Algeria would therefore deliberately seek to recreate that old style of warfare, antedating the institution of the battle as its central act, which characterized hostilities between peoples in the distant past. Their decision, though committing the populations they sought to lead to unspeakable suffering, had the remarkable effect of frustrating their opponents' far greater military power and leading eventually to victory. Meanwhile, the greatest of the industrial nations, now known as super-powers, contemplated each other across the frontiers of their ideological empires in the awful knowledge that the ultimate of weapons obliged an agreement never to fight battles again.

The Bayeux tapestry, which may have been commissioned by Bishop Odo, was created as an official commemoration of the campaign of the Norman Conquest of England. This detail [RIGHT] shows the Bishop, Duke William's natural brother, rallying the temporarily disorganized Normans during the Battle of Hastings. He took part in the battle wearing the full armor of a knight but, being in holy orders, carried a mace instead of a sword. The inscription "ODO EPS: BACULV. TENENS" emphasizes the point.

Gilbert was an immensely successful Victorian illustrator, with a romantic enthusiasm for the Middle Ages even more developed than normal for the time. Agincourt [BELOW RIGHT] was a natural subject for an artist of his type, since the story of the triumph of a small English army over great odds contributed greatly to the prevailing national myth and the subject allowed him to indulge a Tennysonian feeling for chivalry, armor, mystic swords and faithful steeds.

The Battle of Marignano (September 13-14, 1515) was an attempt by the Imperial, Papal, Spanish and North Italian armies, with their Swiss allies, to defeat a French invasion of northern Italy. Very hard fought and costly, it was one of the first in which field artillery made its power apparent; it also broke the Swiss as an independent military force in European warfare. The illuminator has nevertheless represented the battle in traditional "glorifying" style [OPPOSITE], with King Francis I of France as the dominant figure on the battlefield.

French or English tapestry, *Bishop Odo at the Battle of Hastings* (detail).

Sir John Gilbert, *The Morning of Agincourt* (detail).

French manuscript illumination, *Francis I at Marignano*.

... The perriers battered the walls incessantly night and day; the King of France had one called Male Voisine; but in Acre was Male Cousine [another machine built by the Moslems and so named by the Franks] which was always damaging it, and he [the King] had it constantly repaired; and it was so well repaired that it shattered the principal wall and also caused much damage in the Accursed Tower. The Duke of Burgundy's perrier did its work equally well. The one belonging to the good Knights of the Temple struck many Turks on the head; that of the Hospitallers delivered blows that satisfied everyone. A perrier called the Perrier of God had been set up. To get it made, a good priest collected so much money, by sermons that heartened the whole army, that it was big enough to demolish more than two perches [11 yards] of the wall near the Accursed Tower.

Ambroise, a Norman chronicler,
on the use of siege engines at Acre, 1190.

Indian manuscript illumination, The Armies of the
Pandavas and the Kauravas *(detail).*

Paolo Uccello, *Battle of San Romano*.

"The Mahabharata," greatest of the Hindu epic poems, tells the story of the war between the cousinly families of the Pandavas and Kauravas, which resulted in an eighteen-day battle and the extinction of the Pandavas. Dating from at least 400 B.C., it has been endlessly retold and is still current in India. This seventeenth-century illumination [OPPOSITE] by a Hindu artist portrays the beginning of the battle, with the armies dressed and equipped in the Moghul style of the time.

San Romano, fought on June 1, 1432, was a small action between the Siennese and the Florentines, the latter commanded by their Captain-General, Niccolo de Tolentino, in one of the repetitious Italian city-state wars of the fifteenth century. Its fame derives from the three studies made of the subject by Uccello, the great experimenter with the problem of perspective. All were painted for the palace of the Florentine head of state, Lorenzo de Medici. This [ABOVE] remains in the city; the other two are in Paris and London.

Flemish tapestry, *Battle of Pavia* (detail).

Pavia, February 24, 1525, reversed the result of the Battle of Marignano. Francis I, who personally led the French cavalry in a series of charges, was defeated by the Imperial army, which deployed its Spanish arquebusiers to great effect. The tapestry [ABOVE], made in the Imperial territory of the Netherlands, is a frank celebration of the Emperor Charles V's victory. But the treatment is not unrealistic, the details of armor and armament being meticulously reproduced.

In 1274 and 1281 the all-conquering Mongols attempted to extend their power from China to Japan. The first expedition appears to have been a reconnaissance in force. But the second was a full-scale invasion, defeated by the ferocious resistance of the Japanese and then by a "divine wind" which scattered the Mongol ships. The "divine wind" — kamikaze — gave its name to the Japanese suicide air attacks of the Second World War. This scroll painting [BELOW], executed shortly after the repulse of the invasions, is of warriors gathering in a fortress to defend the country.

Bahadur, the son of vassals of the Moghuls, made himself independent ruler of the Kingdom of Malwa, in Central India. He continued to reign independently after his father's death, but in 1564 surrendered the state to the Emperor Akbar. This sixteenth-century illumination [RIGHT] discloses many details of Moghul warfare of the period, including the use of elephants in the line of battle and the beating of kettle drums to strike fear into the enemy.

Indian manuscript illumination, *Capture of Bahadur Khan* (detail).

Moko Shurai Ekotoba, *Repulse of the Mongol Invasions* (detail).

This eighteenth-century engraving [ABOVE] is of one of a series of ten tapestries, woven in Delft by Cornelis Vroom and finished about 1619, which were commissioned by Lord Howard of Effingham as a national memorial to the victory of 1588. Most were burnt in the fire of 1834, which destroyed the House of Lords where they had been hung by Cromwell. It shows the two fleets off Calais after their week-long running battle up-Channel.

This is a characteristic Dutch sea-scape battle picture of a notable incident of the Anglo-Dutch War [OPPOSITE ABOVE].

Turner, over a long life and enormous output, worked in at least four successive styles, beginning with that of the Dutch seventeenth-century marine artists and ending, via classicism and romanticism, with proto-impressionism. This highly Romantic view of Trafalgar [RIGHT], which shows *Victory* boarding *Redoutable* at the climax of the battle, is accurate in detail even if over-dramatized in mood. The *Victory*'s two flags at main masthead form the signal for "Close Action" that Nelson kept flying throughout the fighting.

J. Pine, *The Defeat of the Spanish Armada*.

Abraham Storck, *The Battle of the Texel*.

J.M.W. Turner, *The Battle of Trafalgar*

I am at present towing the *Victory* and the Admiral has just made the signal for me to go with her to Gibraltar, which is a satisfactory proof to my mind that he is perfectly satisfied with Old *Neptune*, who behaves as well as I could wish. The loss of Nelson is a death blow to my future prospects here..., and I am aware that I shall never cease to lament his loss whilst I live. We have ten Men killed and 37 Wounded, which is very trifling when compared to some other Ships, however we alone have certainly the whole credit of taking the *Santissima Trinidada*, who struck to *us alone*. Admiral Villeneuve was with me on board the *Neptune* over two days, I found him a very pleasant and Gentlemanlike man, the poor man was very low! Yesterday I put him on board the *Euryalus* with Admiral Collingwood, but I still have the pleasure of feeding and accommodating his Captain and his 2 Aid du Camps and his Adjutant General, who are true Frenchmen, but with whom I am much amused, I have also 450 poor Spaniards from the *Santissima Trinidada*, with a true Italian priest born at Malta, – I have found an excellent French cook and a true Spanish pug dog....

Captain Thomas Fremantle
writes to his wife Betsy
from his ship Neptune, *October 28, 1805,*
a week after Trafalgar.

Unknown, *The Battle of Lepanto*.

Ken Sai Naga Toshi, *The Battle of the Yalu*.

An excellent "analytical" painting of the decisive sea battle between the Christian and Turkish fleets [LEFT]. The Christian galley in the foreground has driven its ram into the side of her Turkish opponents and the two fighting crews are exchanging fire from the platforms (*arumbada*) above the main battery.

The Sino-Japanese War of 1894-5 was provoked by Japan to wrest from China control of her vassal state of Korea. The battle of the Yalu (September 17, 1894) was fought to allow the passage of the Japanese invasion fleet and was a complete Japanese victory, due largely to the superiority of their British-built ships. It is a tribute to the skill of this woodcut artist that he has adapted an entirely traditional medium to a steam age subject [ABOVE].

Early at the break of day, the bombard-ment began again from the enemy side even more horribly than before. They fired from all redoubts without stop-ping. Our detachment, which stood in the hornwork, could scarcely avoid the enemy's bombs, howitzer shot and can-non balls any more. No one saw nothing but bombs and balls raining on our whole lines.

Early this morning the English light infantry returned from Gloucester and mounted their post in the hornwork again. They said it would be impossible to break through there, because every-thing was strongly garrisoned and entrenched all the way around by the enemy; also there was a cordon drawn by some squadrons of French Hussars about the whole region, so that nothing at all could pass in and out any more.

Also, this morning right after reveille, General Cornwallis came into the hornwork and observed the enemy and his works. As soon as he had gone back to his quarters, he immediately sent a flag of truce, with a white standard, over to the enemy. The light infantry began to cut their new tents in the hornwork to pieces and many were altogether ruined, so one expected an early surrender.

Johann Doehla, a Hessian in British service, at the Siege of Yorktown, October 17, 1781.

Flemish tapestry, *Oudenarde* (detail).

This tapestry [ABOVE] from the set at Blenheim Palace commemorating Marlborough's vic-tories in the War of the Spanish Succession shows Marlborough supervising the course of battle (July 11, 1708) against the French army under Marshal Vendome. The figures on his left and right are the Elector of Hanover and Prince Eugene. In the corner an allegorical figure representing the River Scheldt holds a plan of the fortress of Oudenarde. The tapestries were probably designed by Lambert de Houdt, who had earlier created a famous series called the *Art of War* purchased in different versions by the Electors of Bavaria, the Grand Duke of Baden and King William III of England.

After Daniel Maclise, *The Meeting of Wellington and Blücher* (detail).

This engraving [LEFT] is one of two great murals for Barry's new House of Lords executed after Maclise on patriotic subjects. (The other is of the death of Nelson). This detail portrays, in high Romantic style, Highlanders and British infantry tending wounded cavalrymen at the close of the Battle of Waterloo. In the background Wellington's heavy cavalry escort, bearing a captured French eagle, witness the meeting of the Allied generals.

A naive contemporary copy of a well-known watercolor of Wellington during the course of the battle [BELOW]; the tree trunk on the left is the one at the crossroads at the center of the battle line, near which Wellington spent much of the day.

After John Augustus Atkinson, *The Battle of Waterloo* (detail).

Louis François Lejeune, *The Battle of Borodino*.

Louis François Lejeune, *The Battle of Somo Sierra* (detail).

Lejeune was a professional soldier as well as a painter who achieved the rank of general under Napoleon. He specialized in large battle scenes, which combined faithful rendering of event and topography with careful celebration of the role of the leading figure present. Some Sierra, November 30, 1808, was a rearguard action by a small Spanish army under General San Juan, fought to check the French advance on Madrid [ABOVE].

Borodino, otherwise known as the Moskowa, was fought by Napoleon (September 7, 1812) to carry the Russian entrenched position astride his route of advance to Moscow. The scene [ABOVE TOP] shows Marshal Berthier, Napoleon's chief of staff, returning a captured Russian general's sword as a token of courtesy. In the right rear, General Caulaincourt leads his infantry in an assault on the Russian Great Redoubt.

Louis François Lejeune, *The Battle of Aboukir*.

Napoleon's invasion of Egypt in 1798 attracted a counter-offensive by a Turkish army, under Mustapha Pasha, brought by British ships from the island of Rhodes. It was met on landing by Napoleon, who defeated it in a short battle at Aboukir, July 25, 1799. Lejeune's painting [ABOVE BOTTOM], also from his Versailles series, shows Mustapha surrendering to Murat, Napoleon's light cavalry leader.

American lithograph, *Battle Between the Monitor and the Merrimac*.

Peter Rothermel, *The Battle of Gettysburg* (detail).

Lee's last invasion of the North culminated in his interception by the Union army, under General George C. Meade, at Gettysburg, Pennsylvania, and a murderous battle, July 1-3, 1863, in which the Confederates were decisively beaten. Rothermel's canvas [ABOVE] represents, with a great deal more feeling than documentary accuracy, the repulse of Pickett's charge on the third day, the moment that decided the outcome of the battle and perhaps of the American Civil War.

This engagement was famous both as the first between ironclad steamships and the last in which the Confederacy tried to break the Union stronghold on its sea lanes. On March 8 the *Merrimac* devastated the Union squadron of wooden walls blockading the Virginian ports. Next day the *Monitor*, which fortuitously happened to be ready for sea, arrived from New York and engaged her [OPPOSITE]. The duel was inconclusive but the *Merrimac* did not again contest the issue. The *Monitor* gave its name to a class of bombardment ships for which navies continued to find a use long after ironclads had developed beyond the embryo form this vessel represented.

Accordingly on the morning of the twelfth very early the cannonading began. Sumter was silent until after breakfast when she responded east and west to Moultrie, the floating battery, and the batteries on Morris Island. Steadily the bombardment continued all day and all night without a casualty on either side. On Saturday the U.S. fleet with the expected reinforcements arrived off the harbour. Then the firing redoubled! Sumter signaled violently to her friends for aid – fought with her colours at half mast! Yet no aid came! Her flag is down! Has she surrendered? No, shot down by one of the batteries. Again she signals for assistance. Shame on the dastard Navy outside! So wore on the day. One chivalrous act I must mention. When the flag was shot down admidst the thickest of the fight, through the smoke of battle went a little boat with another U.S. flag for their enemy to fight under! Was ever anything handsomer?

Mrs. Catherine Edmondson, an eye-witness of the bombardment of Fort Sumter which opened the American Civil War, April 15, 1861.

Fripp's doomed heroes [BELOW] are the remnants of the 24th Foot, South Wales Borderers, about to be overwhelmed by Cetewayo's Zulu *impis*. The battle (January 22, 1879) was one of the two great disasters suffered by white armies in Africa during the nineteenth century. Unlike Adowa, where the Ethiopians massacred an Italian army by superior generalship in 1896, the defeat was the result of a simple failure to distribute ammunition. Both battles, however, stemmed from rash imperialist adventures. Fripp was a professional war artist, who covered many wars for the London *Graphic* between 1878 and 1905 and died as a result of hardships suffered in the Russo-Japanese War of 1904-5.

Caton Woodville, an even better-known professional war artist than Fripp, worked for the *Illustrated London News* from 1878 until the First World War; his efforts to impose the imagery of the traditional battle-scape on the scenery of trench warfare in 1914-15 produced some of the most grotesque examples of military art ever published. Here [OPPOSITE], at the Alma, he is at home: the scene, an imaginative reconstruction, represents the color party of the Coldstream Guards attacking the Russian line in the opening battle of the Crimean War, September 20, 1854.

C.E. Fripp, *The Battle of Isandhlwana.*

Robert Caton Woodville, *Heights of Alma, Storming the Great Redoubt* (detail).

Japanese woodcut, *The Storming of Weihaiwei*
(detail).

Toshihida, *Japanese Gun in Action* (detail).

Utaban Kuniyoshi, *The Revenge of the Soga Brothers*.

This contemporary woodcut [OPPOSITE] is of one of the decisive incidents of the Sino-Japanese War, January 30, 1895. The European clothing of the Japanese, in a scene otherwise wholly traditional, hints at the explanation of their easy success over the Chinese who, though equipped with European artillery, were quite outclassed by the modernized army of their island neighbors. Weihaiwei was one of the prizes that Japan was forced to cede to the great powers (in this case to Britain) as a condition of their settlement of the war.

A three-panel woodcut of the Russo-Japanese War [ABOVE]; the gun crew is serving one of the German Krupp pieces of a field-battery, with infantry moving up to the attack in the background.

The Sogas became the dominant clan in sixth-century Japan when they espoused Buddhism and established it as the national religion. This swordsman in violent conflict during a night attack by the Sogas on the murderers of their father [RIGHT] is by one of the leading nineteenth-century Japanese woodcut artists, a pupil of the great Toko-yuni, who specialized in warrior subjects.

Sioux Chief Red Horse,
The Battle of the Little Big Horn (detail).

Paul Kane, *The Death of Big Snake, Blackfoot Chief.*

Frederic Remington, *Cavalry Charge*.

This pictograph [OPPOSITE ABOVE] by an Indian participant in the destruction of Custer's 7th Cavalry column at the Little Big Horn, June 25, 1876, represents the whole course of the massacre in a single scene. Custer, attempting to drive the northern Sioux under their chief, Crazy Horse, onto their assigned reservation, impetuously attacked with inferior numbers. He and his 212 men were all killed.

A romanticized view of Red Indian warfare [OPPOSITE BELOW]. Though the picture was done for popular taste, the artist had travelled extensively in the American West.

Remington hero-worshipped the "Indian-fighting army," which he accompanied on many of its campaigns in the American West. A gifted sculptor as well as painter, his studies of cavalrymen [ABOVE], Indians and cowboys were much influenced by the sequential photographs of Isaacs and Muybridge (1872), which for the first time revealed how animals actually moved.

Seeing his men's predicament, Captain Haupt, who had just reached the barbed-wire entanglements, shouted: "We'll take the fort by assault!" In such perilous circumstances, his words sounded like a bad joke. Already, however, some men were busy cutting the wire with shears, and soon had opened a few gaps. The Brandenburgers stumbled over the tangle of wires, only to run into the still greater barbed-wire network set up immediately around the fort.

Not a shot came from the fort, all was deathly quiet. What was going on inside? Had the fort been evacuated or were the French prevented by our artillery from firing on us? Or, again, was there such a confusion in the fort that the French were unaware of the enemy's presence?...

Our captain was weighing the risks. With every passing minute, however, they would become greater. An immediate and fully conscious decision was called for. Standing upright in the trench, his cane held high, the captain shouted: "Forward! The fort is ours! Fall who must!" Some men followed him, others, undecided, held behind. He came back toward them, and exclaimed: "My boys! You are not going to let me down, are you?"

Walter Bemmelberg at the taking of Fort Douaumont, February 25, 1916.

John Nash, *Over the Top*.

John Nash, a brother of Paul, was also influenced by the Cubists, as this picture of the Artists' Rifles attacking from a trench at Marcoing in the Cambrai Salient on December 30, 1917 reveals. Unlike his brother, he was not an Official War Artist, but a serving soldier in the regiment.

Dwight Shepler, *Battle for Fox Green Beach*.

We flew in a V of Vs, like a gigantic spearhead without a shaft. England was on double daylight-saving time, and it was still full light, but eastward, over the Channel, the skies were darkening. Two hours later night had fallen, and below us we could see glints of yellow flame from the German anti-aircraft guns on the Channel Islands. We watched them curiously and without fear, as a high-flying duck may watch a hunter, knowing that we were too high and far away for their fire to reach us. In the plane the men sat quietly, deep in their own thoughts. They joked a little and broke, now and then, into ribald laughter. Nervousness and tension, and the cold that blasted through the open door, had its effect upon us all.

Major-General Matthew B. Ridgway
on his flight to Normandy,
dawn of D-Day, June 6, 1944.

Sato Kai, *The Bombing of Clark Field*.

Charles Cundall, *The Withdrawal from Dunkirk*.

An American combat artist's view of the Normandy landings, June 6, 1944 [OPPOSITE]. Fox Green was the easternmost of the American beaches. Elsewhere in the same OMAHA sector the Americans suffered heavy casualties; here, landed by mistake half a mile east of their assigned sector, the assault troops got ashore easily and quickly pushed inland.

Clark Field was the main American air base on the Philippines and suffered attack by the Japanese ten hours after Pearl Harbor, Hawaii, December 8, 1941 [LEFT]. Despite the warning, the local American commander had not dispersed his aircraft and most were caught on the ground and destroyed for trifling Japanese loss. The fall of the Philippines was a direct consequence.

The evacuation from the Dunkirk beaches recreated by a well-known Royal Academician [ABOVE]. Between May 28 and June 4, 224,000 British and 112,000 French soldiers were brought off the French coast by a scratch armada of naval ships and small craft and conveyed to England. The artist exaggerates the intensity of the air fighting; the Royal Air Force succeeded in keeping the Luftwaffe at a distance.

The bombing of the Basque town of Guernica by the Nationalist air force on April 25, 1937 caused not only extensive civilian casualties but international outrage. It was the first deliberate bombing of a civilian target in warfare. Picasso's painting, done for the Republic of Spain's pavilion at the Paris Exposition of 1937, was intended both as a work of anti-Nationalist propaganda and a condemnation of the brutality of war in general. Its themes include many favored by Picasso, and it has even been suggested the picture was composed before the raid and that the artist was looking for a title.

Pablo Picasso, *Guernica*.

VII
Armageddon

Pieter Breughel, *The Triumph of Death* (detail).

The Norse vision of paradise was a battlefield on which warriors struck down by the enemy were instantly restored to life so that — so great was the Vikings' enjoyment of fighting — they might at once return to the fray. It is unsurprisingly not one which has a counterpart in the mythic life of any other people, for the majority of whom death in battle, however gloriously achieved, is an ordeal which the individual is expected to undergo only once.

Glory, moreover, is a fickle visitor. The successful conqueror can usually command its presence, even if conjured up retrospectively by the artistry of his court painters and poets. But it is a lucky hero who falls facing fearful odds in full view of spectators with time and talent to record the circumstances. Death in battle is, for the vast majority of those who suffer it, lonely, terrifying and obscure, a fate shunned by all but the most bellicose individuals and peoples. A particular reason for the abhorrence attached to it is the likelihood that the fallen will not receive decent burial or permanent memorial. For even though it is in most cultures a point to honor to recover from the field of battle the bodies of one's dead, the historical probability is that most victims have been buried or cremated unceremoniously on the spot or left to decompose where they fell. One of the worst horrors of the Grand Army's retreat from Moscow in 1812 was to find on retraversing the site of Borodino that the only attendants of the dead they had left there two months before had been the crows and the wolves. And the excavation of the mass grave of the dead of the Battle of Visby in 1361, on the island of Gotland, implied a charnelhouse aftermath quite as awful as anything imagined by Breughel.

The wars of the past have nevertheless left us some notable memorials to their dead, of which Simonides' epitaph on the Three Hundred at Thermopylae — "Go tell the Spartans, thou who passest by/That here obedient to their laws we lie" — has become the most famous. Roman military graveyards yield touching memorials to long-service legionaries killed in action and in more modern times, particularly since the Napoleonic wars, it has become customary to erect memorials to the dead of regiments or nationalities who died on particular battlefields. Every visitor to Waterloo must remember the mound surmounted by the Brabant lion raised by the Belgians to

In a theme directly opposite to that of resurrection, Brueghel's soldiers are locked in vain combat with the forces of destruction.

The entire canvas is reproduced on page 210.

their soldiers who fell there in June, 1815. It was not until the First World War that it became the practice, however, to provide a memorial for each soldier whose body was recovered for burial, a departure necessitated by the claims advanced by the governments of almost all the combatant powers that the war was an expression of the popular will. First to undertake the comprehensive commemoration of their soldiers' sacrifice was the British government, and their war cemeteries have become something of a model for those of all other nations. Their design was entrusted to the leading British architect of the day, Edwin Lutyens, and the choice of words for the common inscriptions to the British Empire's unofficial poet laureate, Rudyard Kipling.

No one who visits the Imperial (now Commonwealth) War Graves Commission's cemeteries is likely to forget the impression of beauty and pathos that it leaves. Each is designed as a garden, planted with "dwarf lupines, nasturtiums, linarias and eschscholtzias, alyssum and candytuft," with roses, pinks and saxifrage as borders to the rows of uniform white headstones. At one end of each cemetery stands a Cross of Sacrifice; it is faced from the other by a Stone of Remembrance bearing the words, "Their Name Liveth for Evermore." Over seven hundred and fifty of these cemeteries were built to shelter the dead of the First World War in France and Belgium alone, and their construction undoubtedly helped give comfort to the parents and wives of the million unreturning.

But no memorial, however dignified, can compensate its subject for the manner of death which most soliders have always suffered. A clue to what that death was in the First World War is provided by the scale of the memorials to the missing: that at the Menin Gate in Ypres records 54,000 names, that at Tyne Cot on the Somme 74,000, that on Gallipoli, which faces the site of Troy across the Dardanelles, 20,000. These were men whose bodies were reduced to fragments by shellfire, or who were buried alive in collapsed trenches, or who drowned in the liquid mud of shell holes or who expired of their wounds in an unregarded corner of the battlefield and were found later only as skeletons, if at all. The naval memorials at Portsmouth, Plymouth and Chatham recall men who died of exposure in the waters of the North Sea or were taken down to its bed in the watertight compartments of their stricken ships. Many of the airmen commemorated fell to their deaths without parachutes or were burned in their flaming machines.

Yet the soldiers of the First World War, for all that they died in numbers greater than in any previous war, were in an individual sense more fortunate than any who had offered their lives on a battlefield before. The weapons which they faced were of a greater lethality than those of the gunpowder or arrow eras. But the medical care which they could hope to enjoy if they could be got from the place of wounding to first aid offered a chance of recovery none of their predecessors had known. Antiseptic dressings and anesthetics saved the lives of thousands, perhaps millions, who would have certainly died at Waterloo, Hastings or Cannae. In the Second World War antibiotics and blood transfusion offered the chance of recovery to almost all who could be got to hospital.

In the millennia of warfare which preceded these innovations, the severely wounded soldier and sailor might be counted as good as dead from the moment he was hit, and many of the lightly wounded would succumb also. For battlefields yield few clean wounds. The passage of a weapon or missile through the soldier's clothing carries germs into the wounds they cause as a matter of course, and the wounds are further infected when the victim falls to the ground. Most weapon wounds, moreover, are by their nature severe, precipitating bleeding which carries the wounded man quickly into shock, against which primitive medicine could provide no remedy. And early surgery was frequently defeated by missiles, which could not be extracted from their final site within the body, or only at the risk of adding to the injury already caused. That was particularly the case in wooden sailing ship warfare, where cannon balls scattered jagged splinters which were much more feared as wounding agents than the shot itself.

Even when the wounded were got to care, they might benefit not at all; their lot indeed might very well be worsened. For battles produce what has been called an "epidemic of casualties" which overwhelms the hospital service, so that the doctors are driven to practice triage, a crude separation of those whose wounds will claim an unfair share of the resources and time which can be offered from the less badly hurt. In modern warfare, few are written off. A hundred years ago, the majority might be. And the luckier would still have to survive the wounded soldier's worst enemy, the cross-infections of the hospitals themselves. Because of these factors, military hospitals in the aftermath of a battle were places of horror, often too unspeakable to be described. One of the first men who found words to describe what he saw, the Swiss Henri Dunant, aroused by his account of the human cost of Solferino (1859) a popular outcry so intense that he was enabled by it to found and fund the Red Cross, the first international organization for the relief of suffering in war.

Almost as immediate to the soldier as fear of wounds was fear of death by disease. The First World War was also the first in which battle deaths exceeded those from non-military causes. Hitherto, soldiers had always died in much greater numbers from illness than at the hands of the enemy, even as late as the Boer War of 1899-1902, when enteric fever and dysentery were the main killers. At earlier dates, epidemics could ravage whole armies out of existence. The best known example of that fate is the one which overtook the army of General Leclerc in Haiti in 1801. Sent to put down the rebellion of Toussaint l'Ouverture, it had been reduced by yellow fever in 1803 from 25,000 to 3000 men. The chronicles of medieval warfare record even more staggering sick lists but, because of the notorious exaggeration of numbers which medieval writers practiced, they must be treated with caution. It certainly seems the case, however, that the armies of Gustavus and Wallenstein, which were facing each other outside Nuremberg in 1632, suffered 18,000 deaths from typhus and scurvy and were forced as a result to withdraw without ever having come to battle. Scurvy, strictly an illness of deprivation rather than a disease, was of course the common lot of deep-sea sailors until the discovery of the citrus fruit specific at the end of the eighteenth century. But it also occurred in armies forced to live on preserved rations, which they were often obliged to do during long sieges. And, because of the low standards of hygiene which generally prevailed until the end of the nineteenth century, sieges often precipitated mass outbreaks of parasitic illness, like plague and typhus. Forced to break camp in consequence, the afflicted soldiers then became mass carriers of the infection; another reason, besides the near certainty of pillage and random violence, why the approach of armies was so feared in European life during the troubles of the sixteenth and seventeenth centuries.

Epidemic disease was also a chief enemy of soldiers taken prisoner. Toward the end of the Middle Ages in Europe the custom developed of allowing propertied prisoners to return home on appropriate payment to the captor — "ransom." And in the seventeenth century ransom gave way to the practice of exchange, by which officers of equal rank were swapped, meanwhile living freely on parole until the negotiation could be completed. Sometimes by "convention," whole captured armies might be released for repatriation. But the common lot of prisoners has always been confinement, if indeed not enslavement. Barbarians commonly enslaved their prisoners, when they did not kill them, as did the Romans. The medieval practice of ransom itself rested on the idea that the prisoner was his captor's possession and had to be bought back, and in colonial warfare the Europeans continued to enslave their captured enemies almost until the abolition of the institution in the nineteenth century. European prisoners in modern times have not been enslaved. But, when it has not been possible to force them to change sides (a favorite recruiting method until the end of the eighteenth century), they have been imprisoned in stockades, fortresses or hulks. And there bad food and overcrowding resulted in mass fatalities with depressing frequency. The sufferings of Union prisoners confined in the Andersonville camp became one of the scandals of the American Civil War, and the outrage it provoked helped give general currency to a code of prisoner treatment, first drawn up by the American Professor Lieber and then accepted at an international conference in Brussels in 1874. Subsequent extension of the Geneva Convention of 1864 to provide for the care of prisoners did much to alleviate their lot. But its observance depended ultimately upon the goodwill of the captor which might often be withheld, as it was on an inhuman scale during the Second World War. Then, of five million Russians who fell into German hands, four million died of starvation, disease or mistreatment. And the Japanese, who cleaved to a warrior code which held men who offered their surrender contemptible, worked thousands of their European prisoners to death.

Victims even more numerous were the hundreds of thousands of fellow Asians whom the Japanese enrolled for forced labor. And they had their counterparts among the East Europeans of whom the Germans brought in millions from the occupied territories to man the war industries of the Reich. Overworked and underfed, many succumbed to hardship before the advance of the Allied armies could release them. Others died as the unintended victims of the Allied campaign of bombing against the German homeland. Instituted originally as a means of bringing war production to a halt by the destruction of key targets in pinpoint raids, it was progressively transformed into a wholesale attack on German cities as the Allied air forces found themselves unable to hit their chosen objectives with the necessary precision. The justification adopted was that "civilian morale" was as important, in a war between industrial nations, as that of the armies which the civilian workforces supplied, and the breaking of the spirit of a population therefore as legitimate an activity as the defeat of an armored offensive or a submarine campaign. And, in strictly strategic terms, the argument may have had foundation. Viewed across the perspective of European history, however, it must be seen as a deplorably regressive step.

It is the hallmark of primitive and barbarian warfare that those who suffer worst by it are the weakest — women, children, the old and the wounded. One of the most important achievements of the Christian church was, during the Middle Ages, to propagate a view of military behavior which held violence against these categories to be dishonorable. And, though not without shameful departures on many occasions, the concept of "non-combatant status" grew in scope and acceptance throughout the centuries which followed. A result much remarked was that during the eighteenth century, civilians freely visited the territory of countries with which their own were at war without suffering or fearing interference in any way; their immunity derived from the very fact that they were civilians. Armies, if at all properly controlled, exercised a similar restraint in their dealings with foreign populations even when on campaign. As late as the First World War, and despite much effort by sensation-seeking journalists to show evidence to the contrary, the incidence of atrocity against civilians in occupied territory was almost nil. Thirty years later it had become commonplace. Two and a half million Russian civilians died during the Second World War, many the victims of privation, but a considerable proportion as a result of campaigns of extermination directed against partisan bands but conducted without discrimination for age or sex. Similar atrocities were committed throughout eastern Europe wherever the Germans encountered guerrilla resistance.

The Allies professed outrage at these acts. When enemy propaganda counter-charged that they themselves were guilty of terror against civilians through their strategic bombing campaign, they disclaimed guilt by alleging they were responding to raids which the Germans had initiated. Original sin in the matter is difficult to establish. What is certain is that the scale of civilian death achieved by the Allies exceeded anything inflicted on their own populations. German bombs killed 60,000 British civilians during the war. Allied bombs killed 300,000 Germans and 500,000 Japanese. Among the latter, over 100,000 died in the two attacks on Hiroshima and Nagasaki in August 1945, attacks in which uranium and plutonium bombs were used.

The military and civilian leaders of Germany and Japan were tried as war criminals in 1946, and the more important ones executed. The justice of the verdicts, in so far as they related to the deliberate extermination of civilians, particularly of the European Jews in German concentration camps, is not disputed. But it is now widely recognized that the Allies, by their adoption of a policy of mass destruction of civilian targets, severely compromised their claim to moral superiority over their enemies. And, more seriously, that they set back by so doing centuries of effort to invest the conduct of war with standards of restraint and forebearance. Moral extremists, who see all warfare as criminal, decry that effort as a hypocritical mitigation of an activity which civilized states should shun altogether. Civilized realists, who accept that universal peace must wait upon the reformation of human nature, regret every inch by which the liberal societies of the world have retreated from the standards of military conduct which they preached and, to a considerable extent, practiced during their all too short years of self-confident idealism in the nineteenth century.

Brueghel's surrealist vision of the fate of sinners [RIGHT] is apparently a sermon in paint, but it has also been interpreted as visual propaganda against the harshness of Spanish rule in the Netherlands and the excesses of Alva's army.

Raemaekers, a Dutch artist, produced a stream of highly effective polemical cartoons during the First World War. The theme here [OPPOSITE] is anti-war in general, but his message was violently anti-German for the most part, and he moved to London to carry on his work more easily. He also enjoyed the enthusiastic patronage of the British government.

Pieter Breughel, *The Triumph of Death*.

Louis Raemaekers, *To Your Health, Civilisation*.

Stanley Spencer, *Resurrection of Soldiers* (detail).

Albrecht Dürer, *Four Horsemen of the Apocalypse*.

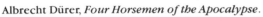

The slope...was littered with dead, both theirs and ours. I got to one pill-box to find it just a mass of dead, and so I passed on carefully to the one ahead. Here I found about fifty men alive, of the Manchesters. Never have I seen men so broken or demoralized. They were huddled up close behind the box in the last stages of exhaustion and fear. Fritz had been sniping them off all day, and had accounted for fifty-seven that day — the dead and dying lay in piles. The wounded were numerous — unattended and weak, they groaned and moaned all over the place...some had been there four days already...

Lieutenant W. G. Fisher,
42nd Australian Infantry,
at Passchendaele, Third Battle of
Ypres, October 10, 1917.

Max Klinger, *War*.

Dürer's *Apocalypse* was the first book wholly the work of an artist; he was his own printer and publisher as well as typographer and designer. The *Four Horsemen* of the Apocalypse [OPPOSITE LEFT], the best-known and most powerful of the woodcuts, epitomized the idea of divine retribution in Christian morality.

Spencer had served as a medical orderly on the Salonika front in the First World War and his *Resurrection* [OPPOSITE RIGHT], one of a series of large symbolic works, derives from his experience there. The series was painted as a memorial to a soldier killed in the war.

Klinger's etching [ABOVE] recalls Goya's *Horrors of War* in tone and subject; the figures in the foreground represent Napoleon's Grand Army. The symbolic giant waking from slumber like a dormant volcano is, however, a northern, indeed Wagnerian element.

Paul Nash, *Hill 60*.

What was heart-rending in the day was intolerable at night; and I rose and wrote, at four o'clock in the morning, to the chief surgeon, offering to perform the necessary operations upon the French. At six o'clock I took the knife in my hand, and continued incessantly at work till seven in the evening; and so the second and third day.

All the decencies of performing surgical operations were soon neglected. While I amputated one man's thigh, there lay at one time thirteen, all beseeching to be taken next; one full of entreaty, one calling upon me to remember my promise to take him, another execrating. It was a strange thing to feel my clothes stiff with blood, and my arms powerless with the exertion of using the knife! and more extraordinary still, to find my mind calm amidst such variety of suffering; but to give one of these objects access to your feelings was to allow yourself to be unmanned for the performance of duty. It was less painful to look upon the whole than to contemplate one object.

Sir Charles Bell, Surgeon,
describes the medical aftermath
of Waterloo at Brussels, June, 1815.

Otto Dix, *Flanders*.

Nash here applies his Cubists technique to a trench scene of the First World War [OPPOSITE]. Hill 60, south of Ypres, was a pile of spoil excavated from a nearby railway cutting. In the uniformly level landscape of Flanders it provided a desirable point of observation, though only of sixty meters' elevation, and was much fought over by the British and Germans, particularly in 1915.

A generalized view of the appalling First World War Flanders landscape which, by 1917, shelling had nearly returned to its original state of swamp [ABOVE]. In Dix's expressionist vision all the natural elements – men, trees and barbed wire-like bushes – are slowly being engulfed in the devastation.

Henry Carr, *St. Clement Dane's on Fire after Bombing*.

St. Clement Dane's, a Wren church that stands in the middle of the Strand, was burned out during the London Blitz of 1940 [ABOVE]. Now rebuilt, it is the official church of the Royal Air Force.

Sutherland was appointed an Official War Artist to record scenes of the London Blitz of 1940-1, and his semi-abstract paintings of the destruction wrought by the German bombers are among the most successful of modern anti-war pictures [OPPOSITE ABOVE].

This drawing [OPPOSITE BELOW] was one of those done by survivors of the atomic bomb explosion at Hiroshima on August 6, 1945. Recalling the event in the 1970s, people wrote and drew their memories and experiences, many in an untutored but deeply moving way.

Graham Sutherland, *The City, A Fallen Liftshaft*.

Yasuko Yamogata,
Hiroshima.

The Cossacks at first hauled us along by the tails of our coatees and our haversacks. When we got on foot they drove their lance-butts into our backs to stir us on. With my shattered knee and the other bullet wound on the shin of the same leg, I could barely limp, and good old Fletcher said "Get on my back, chum!" I did so, and then found that he had been shot through the back of the head. When I told him of this, his only answer was, "Oh, never mind that, it's not much, I don't think." But it was that much that he died of the wound a few days later; and here he was a doomed man himself, making light of a mortal wound, and carrying a chance comrade of another regiment on his back.

Private J. W. Weightman describes his capture by Cossacks after the battle of Balaclava, 1854.

Delacroix, whose name, according to Baudelaire, was synonymous with Romanticism, here inveighs in paint against the cruelty of the Turks toward their Greek subjects in general, and in particular against their massacre of Christians at Chios in 1822. In fact, the work is flagrant propaganda; at the outbreak of their War of Independence (1821-32) the Greeks massacred Turks with unbridled enthusiasm.

Eugène Delacroix, *Massacre of Chios*.

Anton von Werner, *Crown Prince Friedrich by the Corpse of General Douai at the Battle of Weissenburg*.

Weissenberg was the second battle of the Franco-Prussian War (August 4, 1870) in which the Crown Prince's army surprised Marshal McMahon's corps and inflicted on it heavy casualties, among them Douai, one of the divisional commanders. Werner's photographic treatment is typical of contemporary German military painting.

My body will soon be dead, but my soul will remain beside you, near the Lord Buddha. Do not weep, Father, Mother, and you, my sisters, I entreat you. I will always be by your side, working, taking my meals, being happy or sad. Autumn will come, the chirping of the crickets, the forest despoiled of its foliage will remind you of my death, but do not weep. Look after your health and be brave. I wish you a long and happy life. The atomic bomb that fell on 6 August had a terrifying power. It caused burns on my face, my back and my arms. I die thanking the doctors, the nurses and all my friends for their kindness.

25 August, 9 p.m.

*Minoru Suzuki,
a victim of the Hiroshima
atomic bombing, writes a
death-bed letter to his parents.*

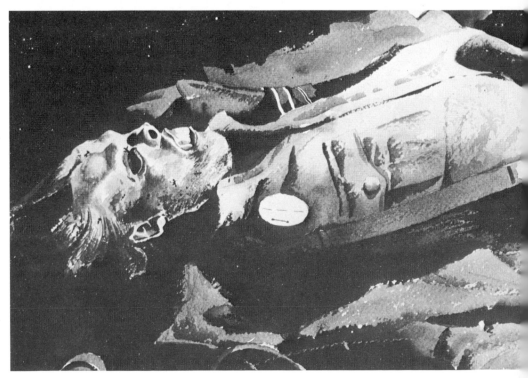

Hans Baluschek, *The Church Window.*

Austin Spare, *Dressing the Wounded During a Gas Attack*.

The widespread destruction of French village churches by long-range artillery fire in 1914-15, inevitably blamed on the Germans, provided much ready-made pictorial propaganda but also occasions for philosophical or sentimental paintings on the incongruity of war and the Christian message [ABOVE LEFT].

Comfort was a Canadian Official War Artist in Italy, where two Canadian divisions served in 1943-5. The Hitler Line [LEFT] was constructed across the western half of the Italian peninsula between Cassino and Rome during the winter of 1943-4. It was broken by the Allies on May 23, 1944.

Spare worked as a medical orderly during the First World War. He recorded his experiences in a series of line and chalk drawings, whose dispassionate accuracy is brilliantly adapted to their subjects [ABOVE].

Charles Comfort, *Dead German on the Hitler Line*.

Sir William Orpen, *A Death Among the Wounded in the Snow*.

Orpen's scene [ABOVE] had all too many counterparts in reality. Like Spare, who turned to
mysticism, Orpen (the leading English portrait painter of his day) was outraged by the
war. In a famous gesture he painted out all
the portraits in a commissioned com-
memorative of the signing of the Treaty of
Versailles and substituted two shell-shocked
Tommies. His action scandalized the Royal
Academy, and the picture was refused by the
Imperial War Museum until a compromise
treatment was agreed upon.

Rogers was an officer of the Royal Army
Medical Corps commissioned to record
medical work during the First World War.
The subtitle to this painting [RIGHT], *in Arduis
Fidelis (Faithful in Hardships)*, suggests the
subject is a stretcher-bearer who has succumbed to gas while transporting wounded.

Gilbert Rogers, *Gassed*.

François Flameng, *Five O'Clock in the Morning, 31.7.17*.

Flameng, a painter employed by the
Musée de l'Armée, specialized in the painting
of uniforms, a preoccupation apparent in this
studio view of French infantry attacking in
Flanders on the first day of the Third Battle
of Ypres (Passchendaele).

Francisco Goya, *Tampoco* from *The Horrors of War.*

The horrors of the Napoleonic Wars in Spain, 1808-14, intensified the strain of the grotesque in Goya's vision. He expressed his feelings about the cruelties inflicted on the Spanish by the French and by the famine they caused in this famous series, executed between 1812-20. *Tampoco* [ABOVE] (which follows a print entitled *One Can't Tell Why*) means roughly "Ditto;" both show Spaniards executed by the French in reprisal for guerilla activity. The second etching is *Esto es Peor,* "*This Is Worse*" [OPPOSITE ABOVE]. The third, *Con Razon O Cin Ella, "With Reason or Without"* [OPPOSITE BELOW], epitomizes the defiance of the country people toward the invaders.

Francisco Goya, *Esto Es Peor* from *The Horrors of War*.

Francisco Goya, *Con Razon O Cin Ella* from *The Horrors of War*.

Jacques Callot, *Execution Scene* from *Grandes Misères de la Guerre* (detail).

Callot, one of the greatest of engravers, specialized in studies of the social scene and human types but turned, as the Thirty Years' War intensified, to anti-military subjects, collected in the series *Grandes Misères de la Guerre*. This scene [ABOVE LEFT] is one of the plates. It is usually held that the target of the series was the French army, since Callot was a Lorrainer and therefore on the opposing side.

Goya's great painting [ABOVE RIGHT] for which some of the *Horrors of War* etchings were studies, commemorates the execution of citizens of Madrid by the French in reprisal for the uprising the previous day against their occupation.

Maximilian, a Habsburg prince, had been installed on the throne of Mexico in 1863 by Napoleon III of France but overthrown and executed by a popular revolution in 1867. Manet appears to have been inspired to paint the scene [OPPOSITE] by his enthusiasm for Goya's *Third of May*; such was his obsession with the theme that he produced four versions. But inevitably, in the illiberal climate of the Second Empire, his choice of subject was seen as a gesture of disrespect and he was forbidden to exhibit it. Manet served as an officer in the Franco-Prussian war in a unit of the National Guard commanded by Meissonier.

Francisco Goya, *The Third of May, 1808*.

Edouard Manet, *The Execution of Emperor Maximilian*.

Käthe Kollwitz, *The Fallen*.

Only a few days ago a Captain of the 11th Welsh died in this hospital. He was mortally wounded in the Battle of Doiran. He is buried near the hospital. Our chaplain decided to hold a short funeral service over the grave; but everyone is busy, and I am only able to collect a few sanitary men and runners. The Captain's name has been neatly painted in good English letters on a white cross. I'm afraid our ceremony is not very impressive. The chaplain is a dear, serious little man, but he does not look well in khaki. The men are dingy and apathetic, and are probably thinking (if they are thinking at all) about something else. Nobody has a prayer book. Nobody knows what the poor Captain looked like when he was alive, and so the ordinary invocation of sentiment or memory is impossible. We only know that he was desperately wounded in the fighting of the 18th, and that he was taken away by the Bulgars to die in their hospital. He was among the "missing."

British Medical Officer at Salonika, September 25, 1918.

Before the First World War, Kollwitz had specialized in the mother-and-child theme but, after the loss of her son in action in 1914, her work became specifically pacifist; this lithograph supposedly represents the mother of a family at the moment of hearing of her husband's death at the front. She was expelled from the German Academy as a "decadent artist" after the Nazi seizure of power. Her grandson was killed in action in 1942.

VIII
Surrender & Aftermath

French manuscript illumination, *The Capitulation of Bordeaux* (detail).

The most dangerous of all moments in warfare is that of surrender, when a combatant literally "gives himself" into the hands of the enemy. Difficult enough a transaction for the commander of an army or head of state to arrange with any confidence that the advantage thus conferred on the enemy will not be unfairly exploited, it must be for the individual fighting man an act of blind trust or desperation. Until the moment he lays down his arms, he himself has been threatening the enemy with death. His captors may still be in the grip of fear or rage, of which he will be the immediate target, and they may very well have lost comrades at his hands. The compunction not to kill or harm him is therefore a weak one, and there is a great deal of evidence that it is not always resisted. On the evening of the battle of Waterloo, for example, Jackson, one of Wellington's staff officers, came across some Prussians busy bayoneting French wounded near Rossomme and saved a British Light Dragoon, over whose unfamiliar uniform they were hesitating, by calling out "*Er ist ein Englander*." Earlier in the day, French lancers had been seen sticking British wounded lying on the ground in front of La Haye Sainte, and on another part of the battlefield British dragoons had sabered some young and unresisting French transport drivers sitting inert on their draft-horses.

Waterloo yields examples of better behavior than this. But, since the blots were in each case on the escutcheon of an army committed to high standards of treatment of prisoners and other non-combatants, we may expect to find in wilder times a more general departure from what had become the rules of warfare at the beginning of the nineteenth century. And the expectation would be fulfilled. The Aztecs of Mexico, a land which they had entered as conquerors from the desert north, brought with them the practice of human sacrifice and ritual cannibalism, to which they were so devoted that their appetite for it could only be satisfied by the capture of prisoners on a vast scale. The Mongols, though not for religious reasons, were also given to the wholesale killing of captives for whom they could not find a use or market, and the slave-trading kingdoms of West Africa, whether or not corrupted by the uncon-cern for human dignity shown by the white buyers, were also given to mass human slaughter. In circumstances like these, no warrior will

The surrender of this last outpost of English power in Aquitaine to the French king on October 19, 1453 marked the end of the Hundred Years' War between the two countries. The illuminator represents the proscribed formalities, in which the bur-ghers begged for their lives and offered gifts, in stylized form.

offer his surrender, and will go down fighting rather than see his women and children fall into the enemy's hands. The extreme warrior cult, characteristic of the Japanese and the Norsemen, probably has its origins in a prevailing pitilessness between enemies.

Most individuals and societies, whatever good reason they saw for taking up arms, do not, however, usually hold it worth a fight to the bitter end. The rituals of surrender are therefore as universal as those of diplomatic rupture, and as stereotyped; indeed, if we look for their origins in animal behavior, probably more so. Modern ethologists have now detected widespread patterns of "submission posture" in the animal world, the counterparts of which are easily recognizable among humans. Defeated in an effort to intrude on an occupant's territory, the intruder will exhibit signs of its acceptance of the opponent's superiority by canceling all physical signals of aggression — erected crests, bristling hair, extended claws — and by exposing some vulnerable portion of its body, which the victor then ignores. Among the higher vertebrates, recourse may even be had to the mediation of a third party, higher-ranking in the social order of the group to which both victor and defeated belong, who perhaps threatens both and then pacifies them by use of accepted gestures of greeting. But for the absence of verbal formulas of surrender and mediation, animal means of terminating disputes therefore closely resemble those of humans.

In individual human combat, and at whatever level of social development, certain signs of submission have universal significance, notably the laying down of arms. Where distance makes that gesture difficult to communicate, it may be symbolized by the display of certain tokens, which in the west in modern times has taken the form of hauling down a ship's flag in naval warfare and displaying a white flag on land — the latter presumably chosen because positive colors have commonly had a belligerent meaning. When the groups involved are of any size, it has become common for messengers from the supplicants to seek a "parlay" with the other side, either to arrange a temporary truce, perhaps for the evacuation of the wounded or the burial of the dead, or to negotiate a full surrender itself.

But battlefield surrenders can rarely be anything but unconditional; all that those admitting defeat can ask is the sparing of their lives, perhaps with the concession of certain attendant dignities, like the right to march into captivity with colors flying and bands playing. More generous terms can be extracted only if the supplicants have calculated the moment of negotiation while certain strengths remain to them: the ability to continue the fight in the open field or the maintenance of an as yet intact fortress wall. Armies still combat-fit may well be able to negotiate their repatriation; Napoleon's army in Portugal in 1808 came to such an arrangement with Wellington at the Convention of Cintra. Besieged but intact fortresses have very frequently been surrendered to the enemy on the understanding that the lives and property of the inhabitants would be spared in exchange for a timely capitulation. Indeed, the ritual of the surrender of fortresses is very ancient. In antiquity it was understood that cities taken by storm became the property of the conqueror, to possess and do with as he chose; conversely, an early surrender laid the basis for a bargain. In the siege warfare of modern times, the rules became yet more strictly stylized. A siege opened with a formal call to capitulate, but its rejection did not obviate the chance to negotiate reasonable terms at a later stage. The making of a "practicable breach," one which offered an entry to the besieger's infantry, was the occasion for the call to be repeated, when it might be accepted on the original terms. Thereafter a successful assault robbed the citizens of all rights. The history of such assaults, like Wellington's at Badajoz in 1812 which resulted in three days of drunken looting and rape, illustrates the wisdom of surrendering in good time.

Fortified cities have often been coterminous with states, which naturally sought a political understanding with the enemy as a condition of ceasing resistance. Surrender in such cases has always taken on a much more complex form than as between combatants in the field. Even among primitive peoples it required several stages for reconciliation to be complete. The villages of the Mount Hagen tribe in New Guinea exchanged pig meat as a first token of willingness to cease fighting, and then vows to war no more. Intermediaries then brought representatives of the two sides together, bearing crossed spears in token of truce. A formal vow was then sworn, the submitting side speaking a line of traditional verse, which was then repeated by the other antiphonally: "The birds Towa and Kopetla shall again leave their footprints behind/Women and pigs shall again go backwards and forwards between us/The trampled grass shall rise again and grow over everything/So shall we again have peaceful relations with each other/We shall live in peace and multiply/We shall make no war on each other." (Vicedom and Tischmer, *The Culture of the Mount Hagen Tribe*.) Finally agreement was reached about reparations.

The good sense of the Mount Hagen people, which stemmed from an acceptance that they must find a way to live with each other, whatever rancor the war has caused, had its counterpart in European diplomacy during the balance of power era from the seventeenth to the nineteenth century. Despite the religious differences and national rivalries of the established powers, all accepted the necessity of sane and generous peacemaking when one side conceded defeat to the other at the end of a war. The attitude was typified at its best by Castlereagh's letter to Lord Liverpool in 1814 over the question of how much booty Britain should extract from her enemies at the end of the Napoleonic wars: "I still feel doubts about the acquisition in sovereignty of so many Dutch colonies. I am sure our reputation on the Continent as a feature of strength, power and confidence, is of more real moment to us than an acquisition thus made." The classical European diplomacy of peace settlement dealt generally in the transfer of territory, colonies, frontier adjustments and surrender of fortresses; it assigned changes of sovereignty and created spheres of influence; it extracted indemnities and even reparations. But it avoided all measures likely to humiliate the pride of nations or monarchs or to foment grievances which might only be healed by a further round of war. The Peace of Utrecht in 1714, which brought to an end the long war between France and her neighbors over the succession to the thrones of England and Spain, was an excellent example of that diplomatic style. All parties conceded something; all gained something. And, but for minor outbreaks, there was no war in Europe for thirty years.

Classical European peacemaking eventually lost its effectiveness when the nascent sense of nationalism in nineteenth century states invested all territorial concessions with a legacy of lasting resentment. Those exacted by the German Empire from France in 1871 caused a bitterness which festered until the outbreak of 1914, and did much to bring it about, while the reordering of German and Russian territory at the end of the First World War implanted dissatisfactions which led directly to its unilateral reversal in 1939. Germany first, and then Russia embarked on a style of war-making which was nakedly imperialist, the intended outcome of which, far from settling differences between states, was to be the abolition of many of the states against which war was opened and the reduction of most of the rest to permanent subordination. Such objects, typical of imperalism since the beginning of recorded history, are indeed inherent in the imperial idea. The Roman Empire, in its drive to achieve what became the fixed frontiers of its dominions, based its diplomatic dealings with defeated peoples on the *deditio*, their affirmation of "total and unconditional submission" to the imperial will. Once made, it conferred on the emperor the right to do with his new subjects whatever he chose. In practice, the option he adopted almost everywhere was to Romanize the conquered and assimilate their customs and institutions. The successive Chinese dynasties adopted the same policy. And both empires also maintained a tributary system over territories beyond the frontiers of direct administration, which allowed them to mount punitive expeditions and exact fresh surrenders whenever their displeasure was evoked. The European empires have been generally less ambitious. Because their conquests were not contiguous with the homeland, they settled for economic and military domination and much less frequently for cultural and institutional assimilation. In India the British even preserved the fiction of an imperial sovereignty separate from that of the British crown. But there, as in French Africa and Spanish and Portuguese America, the exaction of surrender from the conquered differed absolutely from capitulations arranged with enemies at home by reason of the permanent domination it established.

Imperial conquest, because it brought permanent accretion to the wealth and territory of the state, normally conferred on the conquering general the right to enjoy a spectacular reception on his homeward return and extensive personal reward. The division of spoils was not of course necessarily a feature of imperial warfare only. In the British army the distribution of prize money after a European campaign persisted well into the nineteenth century and in the British navy, after the capture of enemy ships, into the twentieth. And, in sanctioning a sharing of the booty, the government was merely perpetuating a feature of victory celebrations as old as war itself, as well as recognizing a primal motivation of combat. It is normal also to celebrate both victory and the return of peace. But the celebration of imperial conquest partook of unusually triumphal qualities. In the Roman republic and empire it was indeed known as a triumph, when the conquering general paraded in state through the streets of Rome to the Capitol. For Scipio's return from victory over Carthage, "trumpeters led the advance and wagons laden with spoils. Towers were borne along representing the captured cities and pictures showing the exploits of war; then gold and silver coin and bullion; then came the crowns that had been given to the general as a reward for his bravery by cities, by allies or by the army itself. White oxen came next and after them elephants and the captive Carthaginian and Numidian chiefs." (Appian)

Execution was frequently the fate of enemy chiefs, once they had played the part of marching before the conqueror's chariot; such was the lot of Vercingetorix after Caesar's conquest of Gaul. Modern Europe came to regard the custom as barbaric — even though practiced by the Spanish in their conquest of South America — and in domestic warfare it progressively came to treat the person of the sovereign as inviolable, an inviolability subsequently transferred to the institutions of government he represented. Between the end of the seventeenth and the middle of the twentieth centuries, therefore, with the exception of Poland, no sovereign government was extinguished in Europe as the result of military defeat. It was because of the outrage felt at Napoleon's breach of that convention that the war against him was prosecuted so unremittingly. In our own times, confronted by enemies whose ideological and imperialist aims threatened the established structure of European order, the old powers revised their view. In the middle of the Second World War, the Allies proclaimed a policy of "unconditional surrender" to be imposed on Germany and Japan after their defeat, and decided after victory to punish the defeated enemy leaders by bringing them to trial as war ciminals. The decision presumed on the one hand a code of international morality which the defeated were held to have violated, and in that sense represented an important legal advance. On the other hand, it could be seen as resurrecting the tradition of conqueror's rights, which three centuries of civilized diplomacy had worked to eliminate.

The mood of the times chose to ignore the legal dubiety of the proceedings because, if with less certain optimism than in 1918, it had fixed on the victory of 1945 as the end of "a war to end war." The popular craving to punish those who had initiated it, and were unarguably responsible for many of its cruelties, was therefore too strong to be denied. Retrospectively, though little regret has emerged for the execution of the enemy leaders, that optimism has waned. The peace of 1918, sustained by a few victor nations which held large areas of the world beyond Europe in imperial subjection, was scarcely broken for twenty years. The peace of 1945, which has led to the dismantling of all the old colonial empires, was broken almost from the outset, first in the Far East, then in the Middle East, subsequently everywhere but in Europe and the Americas. Many of these wars, bitterly fought if small in scope, have drawn in the armies of Europe and America. Most, because of the sponsorship which the parties seek or demand or cannot refuse from the great powers, threaten the general peace. It is preserved between the rich nations by a hair-trigger balance of weapon power, resting on terror rather than a shared belief in the value of peace itself. Among the poor nations, which have little to lose and apparently much to gain by fighting, it is disregarded or despised as a benevolent condition of existence which the haves extend to each other while ignoring the real needs of the have-nots.

Those needs might or might not be met by the money of the great military powers. But, while so much of it is spent on matching each other's armories, the experiment cannot be attempted. Meanwhile, such small resources as the underdeveloped states can muster for national purposes is increasingly devoted to the raising and equipping of armies, which have increased in number in the world since 1945 from thirty to a hundred and forty. Many serve at best to buttress the authority of authoritarian governments. But others are committed to the settlement of disputes with neighbors which the old imperial system masked or failed to solve. All have adopted the doctrine and techniques of the European armies which gave them birth and taught their leaders their trade. Pessimists in the old world may therefore well feel that, while living out a nightmare of peace themselves, they will be condemned simultaneously to watch the new worlds of Asia and Africa stage a repetition of the era of aggression and conquest which Europe had hoped to have put behind it.

S. Drummond, *Admiral Duncan Receiving the Surrender of Admiral de Winter at Camperdown*.

This battle (October 11, 1797) was a hard-fought engagement between the British Channel fleet and the Dutch, then allied to France. Duncan took nine of their fifteen ships, including their flagship. Here [ABOVE], on the quarterdeck of his own *Venerable*, he receives his opponent's sword. De Winter is said to have remarked that it was a marvel "two such giants as Admiral Duncan" and himself should have "escaped the general carnage." Drummond's lively documentary scene includes a powder monkey and captain's servant, right, marine officers, top right, and a gun crew and lieutenant with speaking trumpet, left.

A watercolor by an Official War Artist of a scene from the very end of the Second World War [OPPOSITE].

Edward Ardizzone, *German Villagers Waving White Flags at the Approach of British Tanks*.

Diego Velasquez, *The Surrender of Breda* (detail).

So impersonal, so poor, so barren are those graves! They lie quite close together as if even in death the legionnaires must be drawn up in line for parade. The crosses are so small, so roughly painted, that one cannot get over the feeling that sordid economy is practised even on the last resting-place of the legionnaire. The crosses are hung with wreaths made of glass beads and with an artificial flower here and there. The name of the dead man is written on a small piece of board and underneath the name stands his number. To this comes the laconic addition: "Legion étrangère." I felt sorry for these poor fellows who even in the last sleep of death had to bear a number which reminded one of a convict prison.

Erwin Rosen
at the Foreign Legion Cemetery,
Sidi Bel Abbes, 1910.

Breda, a key fortress in Dutch resistance to Spain during the Thirty Years' War, was forced to surrender on June 5, 1625 after a ten-month siege. Velasquez's picture [RIGHT], which has been called the greatest historical composition ever painted, shows Justin of Nassau offering the key to the fortress to the Marchese Spinola. It was done as one of a series of victory pictures for the Spanish court; others were by Maino and Zurbarán.

Popular hostility to the French occupation of Spain in 1808 forced the most isolated of the occupying armies, under Dupont de l'Etang, to withdraw from Seville toward Madrid. A scratch Spanish army, under de Castanos, cornered Dupont's army at Bailén on July 19 and forced it to capitulate. The scene [OPPOSITE ABOVE] shows the meeting of the two commanders; Dupont has reason to look downcast, as his was the first surrender by a Napoleonic army since Napoleon's rise to power, and the news caused a European sensation.

The surrender of the French to Prussia and her allies in 1871 provided the occasion for the Prussian king's assumption of imperial status within Germany and the foundation of the Second Reich. William I and the Crown Prince, masking the superceded kings, are hailed by their soldiers in Louis XIV's Hall of Mirrors at Versailles, January 18, 1871 [OPPOSITE BELOW]. Behind them rise the colors of the victorious regiments. The center of the stage is dominated by Bismarck and Moltke, political and military architects of the new empire.

José Casado del Alisal, *The Surrender of Bailén*.

Anton von Werner, *Proclamation of the Kaiser*.

Antonio de Pereda, *The Surrender of Genoa*.

Andrea Doria, the Italian admiral, formally offers entrance to his city to the great Spanish admiral, the Marquis de Santa Cruz, on Charles V's cession of his Italian lands to Philip of Spain in 1555 [ABOVE].

A popular woodcut [RIGHT], of news magazine quality, shows the Russian General Stössel surrendering the fortress of Port Arthur to the Japanese Marshal Nogi on January 2, 1905, at the end of a seven-month siege.

Japanese woodcut, *Surrender of Port Arthur*.

Kukryniksi, *Tanya*.

LUNCH HOUR. **There was a general letting off of steam as the defendants met and shook hands and talked for the first time since captivity, some for the first time in their lives. They ate lunch in the courtroom after it was cleared, buzzing with released tension about all sorts of things, from power politics to physical needs.**

As I watched the others eat, several of them remarked that the food was getting better. "I suppose we'll get *steak* the day you hang us," von Schirach grinned.

Streicher was sitting alone, still being snubbed by the others. As I passed him, he stood up to attract my attention. "You know, *Herr Doktor*," he said, trying to make small talk, "I was sentenced in this very room once before."

"Is that so? How many times have you been tried in your lifetime?"

"Oh, 12 or 13 times. I've had lots of trials. That's old stuff."

A little later Ribbentrop buttonholed me again. "You'll see. A few years from now the lawyers of the world will condemn this trial. You can't have a trial without law. – Besides, it's really not nice to let German denounce German as they will at this trial. – That will not make a very dignified impression, mark my word."

The opening day of the Nuremberg War Trials, November 20, 1946, as seen by the prison psychologist, G. M. Gilbert.

An anti-German propaganda painting [ABOVE] by three Russian Socialist Realists, M. V. Kuprianov, P. M. Krylov and N. A. Solokov showing the execution of a girl partisan during the Second World War.

A combination of the symbolic and the highly documentary, this painting [OPPOSITE] shows the dock at the International Military Tribunal at Nuremberg, where the German Major War Criminals were tried in 1946, with scenes evocative of their crimes around them.

Laura Knight, *The Nuremberg Trial*.

Georg Grosz,
The Robbers.

Grosz's drawing [ABOVE] of bankers extorting the savings and trinkets of war veterans is typical of his satirical style. Wildly anti-authoritarian, he was court-martialed for insubordination during the First World War, and fined three times under the Weimar Republic for insulting official institutions or beliefs. His art remains one of the most powerful expressions of individual outrage at the power of the state in this century.

The left-hand panel of the painter's triptych [OPPOSITE LEFT], which "disappeared" from the Dresden Gallery in 1933 upon the Nazi seizure of power, sums up his expressionist feeling for the post-1918 mood of despair and decadence in defeated Germany.

A scroll painting of a scene from the protracted war between the kingdoms of Champa and Annam [OPPOSITE RIGHT], Vietnamese art was heavily influenced by the Chinese.

Vietnamese scroll painting, *The Festive Return of
the Soldiers*.

Otto Dix, *The Sleepwalkers* (left panel).

Peter Paul Rubens, *The Conclusion of Peace*.

Marie de Medici is here seen [ABOVE] in front of the Temple of Concord. This attractive picture hardly corresponds to the historical facts of a turbulent period.

After a nine-year exile, Charles II returned from Holland to England at the invitation of Parliament in 1660. He entered London ceremonially on May 29. This contemporary "analytical" print shows him setting sail from Schevellingen [OPPOSITE ABOVE].

The night of Armistice Day, November 11, 1918, was celebrated with uninhibited enthusiasm in every major Allied city. Here [OPPOSITE BELOW] one of the leading English artists of the period records his impression of the London scene. Crowds are playfully manhandling a captured German trophy gun.

P.H. Schut, *The Departure of Charles II*.

Sir William Nicholson,
Armistice Night
(detail).

Unknown, *Triumphant Return from the Siege of Siena* (detail).

In 1552, the French House of Valois undertook its last invasion of the Habsburg lands in Italy. After defeat at Marciano (August 2, 1553), the French army under Blaise de Montluc was besieged at Sienna, which it was forced to surrender the following year. Here [ABOVE] the Florentine contingent returns triumphantly to its own city.

Henry's entry, after accepting the Catholic faith, marked the effective end of the Wars of Religion, 1560-98. His entry was March 21, 1594. This sketch [OPPOSITE ABOVE] was for a projected series of paintings, never completed, which would have supplemented Rubens' Medici cycle now in the Louvre.

An historical reconstruction of the opening of the reign of the first Habsburg Holy Roman Emperor by one of the founders of the German Nazarene School, whose work strongly influenced the pre-Raphaelites [OPPOSITE BELOW].

Peter Paul Rubens, *The Triumphal Entry of Henry IV into Paris*.

Franz Pforr, *Rudolf of Habsburg's Entry into Basel*.

Charles Fouqueray,
*American Flags on
the Champs Elysées.*

At 11 o'clock sharp, they suddenly surged out of their trenches, shouting and flourishing a red flag, and carrying big signs with the word "Republic" written on them. Many Germans wore a tricolor cockade on their caps. They were all eager to engage in conversation with our soldiers but, to their intense surprise, were disdainfully ignored by them.... Having been rebuffed by our men, the Boches began celebrating the armistice in their own trenches, and in their own way. Throughout the entire sector, they threw grenades away, blew up the ammunition dumps, and in the evening fired all their star shells, illuminating the sky with an incomparable firework display. They also began to sing merry songs and played instruments, apparently not realizing that the armistice meant their country's complete collapse, the deepest humiliation ever sustained by Germany.

*G. Gazier, a French Officer in
the trenches in the Vosges,
November 11, 1918.*

Philip Goul, *The Triumphal Entry of Constantine the Great into Rome* (detail).

A graphic illustrator and poster designer, Fouqueray catches the enthusiasm [ABOVE LEFT] of the French for their American allies in this study of the U.S. color party marching in the July 14 parade in 1919.

A mural painting [ABOVE RIGHT] by a Greek artist showing the emperor entering Rome in 312 after his victory over Maxentius at the Milvian Bridge and acceptance of Christianity.

Luca Signorelli, *The Resurrection*.

This is the third in a series of mural paintings showing the Overthrow of Antichrist, the Destruction of the World, and the Punishment of the Damned and the Ascension of the Blessed. Signorelli's great fresco scene is notable for the vigorous anatomical treatment of the figures, which splendidly suggests the physical as well as spiritual joys of resurrection.

Glossary

11   Limbourg brothers, *Harvest* from *Les Très Riches Heures du Duc de Berri*

This scene of reaping and winnowing on the left bank of the Seine is taken from the Hotel of Nesle, the house of Jean, Duke of Berri in Paris. The towers of the Conciergerie and l'Horloge can be seen in the background, and in the center the Tour Montmorency and Sainte Chapelle. This is the most accurate view known of old Paris, the nearest comparable being that by Fouquet in 1460. The signs of the Zodiac represented are the Twins and Cancer.

15   Edward Hicks, *The Peaceable Kingdom*

One of the artist's paintings of this subject has the following verse inscription:

The wolf did with the lambkin dwell in
    peace
His grim carnivorous nature there did
    cease
The leopard with the harmless kid laid
    down
And not one savage beast was seen to
    frown.
The lion with the fatling on did move
A little child was leading them in love

When the great Penn his famous treaty
    made
With Indian chiefs beneath the elm-tree's
    shade.

22   English book frontispiece, *The Eglinton Tournament*

This extraordinary occasion was inspired by the nineteenth-century taste for the medieval, of which the novels of Sir Walter Scott, especially *Ivanhoe*, are the best example. The participants wore armor, some old, some especially made for the match. The staging was elaborate, and intended for good weather. While the London rehearsal was held in perfect weather, the actual day of the tournament was marred by pouring rain. It is recorded that the King of the Tournament, the Marquis of Londonderry, put up an umbrella over his historic costume, and the tournament was abandoned for several days.

31   Edouard Manet, *The Fifer*

This admirable picture was originally refused by the Paris Salon, which led Zola to write an indictment of the Salon's selection system in *L'Evénement*. Manet was seeking official recognition as a painter, and he did eventually achieve this status with the Legion d'Honneur. This picture was painted early in his career in 1866 before he adopted the palette and technique of his young friends, the Impressionists, for his later and final successes.

35   Henri Rousseau, *Artillerymen*

The group is composed of the gun crew and drivers of a field gun of the 1890s. The men are wearing the blue uniform tunic and white summer trousers. The officer can be distinguished by his triple row of buttons and frogging. The figure on the left is a non-commissioned officer; the man on the right is wearing the fatigue uniform. The gun is the 90 mm model of 1877, which was replaced by the famous 75 mm in 1897.

36   Colored etching, *The Allied Sovereigns at Paris*

The figures are from left to right: Alexander I, Louis XVIII, Franz I, and Wilhelm III of Prussia.

36 German wood engraving, *Austro-Prussian Peace Conference*

The figures are from left to right: Benedetti, Werther, Menagra, Moltke, Bismarck, Wilhelm I, Degenfeld, Karolyi, and Mensdorff.

39 Norman Lindsay, Untitled

The first poster of six Lindsay did for Australia's last recruiting campaign of the First World War. Like some modern cinema advertising, they were posted in sequence, at intervals of seven to ten days. However, before the last two were put up, the armistice had been signed.

40/41 James Gillray, *Political Dreams*

The figures are from left to right: Pitt, Fox, Lord Hawkesbury, Bonaparte, M.A. Taylor,

Windham, Lord Derby, Nicholls, General Walpole, Colonel Hanger, Erskin, Sheridan, Sir F. Burdett, Duke of Bedford, Duke of Norfolk, and Tierney.

42 William Hogarth, *March of the Guards to Finchley*

The print from this picture was dedicated to Frederick II of Prussia, George II having supposedly refused it with the remark: "I hate painting and poetry too! Neither the one nor the other ever did any good. Does the fellow mean to laugh at my guards?" The scene in the picture is near the Tottenham Court Road turnpike: a prize fight is taking place in front of the Adam and Eve public house, while the King's Head opposite is filled with prostitutes, whose mistress, Mother Douglas, has her eyes raised to heaven in prayer.

A subscription for the print entailed a chance of winning the picture. Of 2000 tickets, 1843 were sold. Hogarth gave the remaining tickets to the Foundling Hospital, which won the picture.

The guardsmen are dressed in the uniform illustrated in the *Clothing Book* of 1742, and armed with the Tower Musket (Brown Bess), bayonet and hanger (short sword). The column, which was to halt at Finchley before proceeding to Scotland, was composed of both 1st and 2nd Guards.

51 George Cruikshank, *Peterloo Massacre*

The yeomanry in this picture are uniformed as regular Light Dragoons and armed with the Paget carbine version of the Tower musket, and the 1796 pattern Light Cavalry sword.

56 George Scott, *Buller's Final Crossing of the Tugels*

The gunners are wearing the new khaki service dress, and the Wolseley foreign service helmet, with the artillery grenade in red on a blue patch. The guns, of the twelve-pounder, breech-loading model, were drawn by the teams without gunners on the limber. They rode separately on their own horses in the Royal Horse Artillery.

71 Herbert von Herkomer and F. Goodall, *Earl Kitchener of Khartoum*

The general is wearing Indian-pattern khaki service dress and carries his infantry pattern sword in the frog of a Sam Browne belt, named from its inventor, who devised it after losing an arm in the Indian Mutiny.

75 Jean-Louis David, *Napoleon Crossing the Alps*

The life of David helps to illuminate a whole period of French history and culture. He started as a Rococo artist. In 1785 his picture *The Oath of the Horatii*, in the neo-classical style, was a turning point in his art. The style became identified with republican sentiment in the Revolution, during which David was a deputy. With the fall of Robespierre he was imprisoned. His wife, who had divorced him for political reasons, remarried him in 1798. In that year, partly as an acknowledgement of his wife's intervention and partly as a manifesto of his belief in the antique, he painted *The Sabine Women*. He first met Napoleon in the same year and became his favorite court painter, thus achieving a position as arbiter of taste (some have said dictator) for twenty years. His commissions included Napoleon's splendid coronation scene, which contains more than a hundred portraits. After Waterloo he fled to Brussels, where he died in 1824.

77 H.A. Ogden, *Grant in the Wilderness*

The invention of the telegraph transformed the speed at which information about war could be transmitted. There was no longer much chance that bankers could make financial coups through special intelligence, as the Rothschilds had succeeded in doing by receiving advance news (by pigeon-post) of the outcome of Waterloo. The telegraph enabled the Northern U.S. Army to read in a newspaper about the battle they had fought the day before. As an example of the volume of images produced, Frank Leslie's *Illustrated Newspaper* of New York employed eighty artists, and published more than 3000 illustrations in the four years of war. Sketch pads were issued on which was printed: "An actual sketch made on the spot by one of the Special Artists of Frank Leslie's *Illustrated Newspaper*. Mr. Leslie holds the copyright and reserves the exclusive right of publication."

78 Baron Antoine Jean Gros, *Joachim Murat, King of Naples*

The artist was made a baron by Charles X. Gros had intended to paint the dome of the Pantheon as an apotheosis of Napoleon, but his plan was transformed by political events into an apotheosis of the Bourbons.

84 Peter Paul Rubens, *The Apotheosis of Henry IV and the Regency*

This allegorical composition commemorates Henry IV's assassination: he is seen being helped by Time for his reception on Olympus by Jupiter. Bellona (War) and Victory mourn his death, while wounded hydra Rebellion raises its head. France, represented by nobles, offers "a globe marked with a fleur de lis to Marie de Medici," seated in mourning between Minerva (Wisdom) and Prudence. Sketches for the composition are in Munich and Leningrad.

85 Anne-Louis Girodet de Roucy Trioson *Ossian Receives in Valhalla the Souls of Napoleon's Generals*

The full title from the Louvre catalog reads: "The shades of French warriors conducted by Victory to the palace of Odin are received by the Homer of Septeatrion and by the warlike spirits of Fingal and his descendants." The people represented are Marceau, Kleber, Hoche, Desaix, Dugommier and Joubert. Napoleon, who greatly admired Ossian's poem, also liked the picture. But its romantic character offended David, for he thought the figures insubstantial, and was embarrassed about what to say to Girodet. Sources for the mood of the painting are from Flaxman and Fuseli.

86 Benjamin West, *The Death of General Wolfe*

The scene is not factually correct. The only two figures seen here who were present at Wolfe's death are the young soldier shown holding the flag, Lieutenant Henry Brown, and the soldier on the far left in the green coat who is Volunteer Henderson of the Louisburg Grenadiers. The Indian is a dramatic addition, and all the other figures were elsewhere on the field at the time. The dying general is wearing the scarlet uniform of his rank; the figure on the left, a Colonial irregular, is dressed in a mixture of European and Indian garb. Background scenes include the death of Montcalm. The painting was presented to Canada by the Duke of Westminster through Lord Beaverbrook as a tribute to Canada's role in the First World War.

87   John Singleton Copley, *The Death of Major Pierson*

The dead or wounded officer in the right foreground belongs to the 72nd Highlanders. The infantrymen are mostly grenadiers of the 95th Regiment.

93   Honoré Daumier, *Joyously Singing, Our Brave Troops Move to the Front*

Daumier's liberal opinions were evident from the beginning of his career. When he drew Louis Philippe as Gargantua, he was fined and sent to prison for six months. Most of his graphic work is political satire. Some is satire of French customs and manners. He was a firm enemy of militarism and strongly against re-armament before 1870. After Napoleon III's surrender to the Germans at Sedan, he made a drawing of ruined houses and corpses, giving it as a title the phrase used by Napoleon III in 1852: "The Empire is at Peace."

103   Edouard Detaille, *An Infantry Regiment Halts for Review in the Bois de Boulogne*

The infantrymen are in review order, with the double-breasted blue tunic, red trousers and epaulettes of the line infantry.

105   Gustav Pierre, *Soldiers Marching Off*

These French infantry are in the 1915 horizon blue service dress and the Adrian steel helmet introduced in 1915 to replace the old dark blue and red seen in Detaille's painting on page 103. The rifle is the 8 mm Lebel (1886/93).

105   Chinese silk scroll painting, *Imperial Hunting Party in Manchuria*

It is no accident that the illustrations in this book contain two pictures of huntsmen. As the English poet William Somerville expressed it:

The chase, the sport of kings
Image of war, without its guilt.

107   William Simpson, *The Charge of the Light Brigade*

The artist shows the low hills, which prevented the Light Brigade from seeing the redoubts that they were meant to attack, while the main Russian guns were in plain sight. Lord Cardigan liked the drawing which showed him as prominently leading his brigade, and took it with him to show Queen Victoria.

110   Elizabeth Southerden Thompson, *Scotland For Ever!*

The 2nd Dragoons (Royal Scots Greys) were so named from the color of the horses they rode. They are dressed as dragoons, except for their bearskin caps – a regimental distinction.

115   Kokyo, *Japanese Destroyer Attack at Port Arthur*

By 1904 the traditional woodcut tradition of Japan had largely declined so that this example of the art is from a period of decadence, in which craftsmen were reduced to using their skills for picture postcards.

116   Japanese woodcut, Sea fight

The Sino-Japanese war of 1894-5 created a revival in printmaking, which brought poor and obscure craftsmen out of retirement to fulfill the demands of a new market. The boom finished when peace came.

119   Johann Zoffany, *The Death of Cook*

Zoffany's painting has an additional interest in that it takes sides in a controversy about how Captain Cook died. Some witnesses claimed that he provoked attack. Certainly, he went ashore with a loaded gun, which he discharged. The party of marines with him failed to cover his return to the shore, and he was stoned to death. Zoffany shows the dead man, Lieutenant Phillips who was in charge of the escort, and marines at the water's edge. The anger of the Hawaiians had been roused by Cook's intention to take their king, Terreeoboo, prisoner to ensure the safe return of a stolen cutter. The affair was a case of cultural misunderstanding and sad misjudgement.

130/131   Frank Wooton, *Rocket-Firing Typhoons at the Falaise Gap*

The two knocked-out German tanks in the foreground are Mark VI Panthers.

132   Henry Moore, *Pink and Green Sleepers*

For this drawing there exists a sketch for the composition as a whole and a detailed study of the left-hand head. These are in two sketchbooks, which became known during the war through selective publications; they are now in the possession of the artist's wife, and the British Museum, bequeathed by Lady Clark, the wife of the chairman of the wartime committee responsible for commissioning British artists to record the Second World War. Moore's war drawings were a significant phase of his art, bringing him a wider public and enabling him to rediscover imaginative sources. He was also commissioned to do a series of drawings of miners. ("Britain's Underground Army" was the propagandist description of their job.)

133   Joseph Pennell, *The Ants* from *War Work in the U.S.*

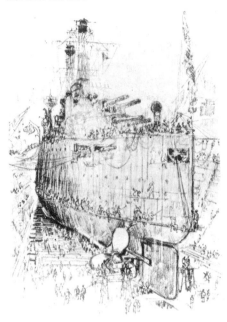

Industrial production being a critical factor in the increasingly technological warfare of the twentieth century, records of industrial activity were used to sustain national morale. This lithograph from Pennell's series of the First World War followed a similar series he carried out in England. Feelings ran deep about the need for soldiers and industrial workmen to be united in purpose, as Rudyard Kipling's couplet from his poem, "Batteries out of Ammunition" reminds us:

If any mourn us in the workshop, say
We died because the shift kept holiday.

142   Indian manuscript illumination, *Akbar Besieges Ranthambor*

The great 16th century Moghul Emperor Akbar had a love of painting that found strenuous expression in patronage. He was illiterate but loved illustrated books: he is quoted as saying, "There are many that hate painting; but such men I dislike. It appears to me as if a painter had a quite peculiar means of recognizing God; for a painter in sketching everything that has life, and devising its limbs, one after the other must come to feel that he cannot bestow individuality on his work, and is thus forced to think of God, the giver of life, and will increase his knowledge."

Akbar's military successes enabled him to recruit foreign artists, who were trained in his Imperial court style. More than a hundred painters worked for him, using a meticulous technique. One of the resulting manuscripts was the illustrated biography of Abu'l Fazl called the *Akbarnama*, now dispersed, but of which more than a hundred leaves are in the Victoria and Albert Museum, London.

144   Jean Fouquet, *Battle Scene*

The miniature comes from a manuscript begun by an anonymous artist working for Jean, Duke of Berri, but completed with eleven miniatures by Jean Fouquet of which this is one. Fouquet was affected by the Italian Renaissance during his visit to Rome in the 1440s, subsequently producing not just book illustrations but miniature pictures of great skill and sensibility. This miniature is an example of the last phase of a great period of European manuscript illuminations during the 1470s, soon to lose ground to the printed book.

154/155   Ernest Meissonier, *Allegory of the Siege of Paris*

A master of historical narrative, Meissonier was devoted to the cult of Napoleon. *1814* is the fourth in a sequence of five pictures he planned, but of which he only painted two, the other being *1807*. In this picture, *1814*, Napoleon is accompanied by Berthier, Duroc, Drouot and Ney in a grim ride to future defeat.

155   Edouard Detaille, *Episode in the Siege of Paris, Villejuif, September 19, 1870*

The soldiers working in the foreground are sappers of the *Génie*; the wide cummerbund worn around the waist was a fashion brought back from the North African campaigns. An artillery gun team waits on the right. Among the spectators on the bank on their right are a hussar, in a fur busby, and a *chasseur à cheval*, in light blue.

159   Jacobo Tintoretto, *Capture of Parma*

One of a group of five paintings recording the exploits of the Gonzaga. The painting demonstrates the gifts of a great muralist.

166   Albrecht Altdorfer, *The Battle of Issus*

One of eighteen paintings in which a famous personality of history or legend represents a particular virtue. It seems that Alexander was chosen as representing military valor. The history of Alexander the Great by Quintus Curtius recorded Alexander's words, the spirit of which is embodied in Altdorfer's painting: "You are not destined to live hemmed in by the rocky crevices and barren glaciers of your home land. The riches of the Orient are spread out at your feet." From the same historical account the painter learned that the battle had ended at nightfall, and chose the clear light of late evening for his exceptional picture.

174   French or English tapestry, *Bishop Odo at the Battle of Hastings*

Not strictly a tapestry, which is woven, but rather an embroidery, this is an invaluable source of information about the eleventh century. The embroidery is nineteen inches deep, more than 230 feet long, and contains 79 scenes.

177   Paolo Uccello, *Battle of San Romano*

Although no portraits are clearly identifiable, the knight unhorsed is believed to be the Sienese commander, Bernadino della Carda.

180/181   J.M.W. Turner, *The Battle of Trafalgar*

This picture, commissioned by George IV, was destined for Windsor Castle. The battle is not represented with accuracy; "a sense of struggle and achievement" was sought instead.

184   Flemish tapestry, *Oudenarde*

The commissioning of a set of tapestries to commemorate the victories of the Duke of Marlborough was part of a national thanksgiving, along with the gift of Blenheim Palace, built specially for him. This is one of eight tapestries.

187   Louis François Lejeune, *The Battle of Aboukir*

Besides Mustapha and Murat three other identifiable figures in the composition are Colonel Duvivier, killed among his dragoons; and Colonel Beaumont attacking a Turk, who is in combat with Adjutant-General Le Turc.

190   C.E. Fripp, *The Battle of Isandhlwana*

The South Wales Borderers are in scarlet home service dress except for the white Wolseley helmet. They are equipped with the Martini-Henry rifle. The cause of the defeat was the failure of ammunition supply for these weapons. This was the result of the regimental quartermaster's unwillingness to break regulations by smashing open the ammunition boxes instead of unscrewing them.

191   Robert Caton Woodville, *Heights of Alma, Storming the Great Redoubt*

Editors in the nineteenth century were convinced that nothing sold a newspaper like a good war. From the 1840s the maxim applied to picture newspapers, of which the *Illustrated London News* was the pioneer. Woodville was an artist who specialized in military subjects. Like other such artists he followed war around the world, sending back drawings that were made into woodblocks by a team of highly proficient engravers.

The guards are wearing home service dress, though the drummer boy has a forage cap instead of a bearskin. The mounted staff officers are in blue undress, and the weapon carried is the 1842 pattern percussion musket.

193   Utaban Kuniyoshi, *The Revenge of the Soga Brothers*

Changes in the subject matter of Japanese prints were determined by the Tempo reforms of 1842, which prohibited the popular themes of actors and courtesans, two main subjects of prints of the golden age, which began in the 1780s. Battle scenes and myths provided alternative themes in the second half of the nineteenth century, and Kuniyoshi is a pre-eminent print maker of the period.

196/197   John Nash, *Over the Top*

The artist remembered the event well and wrote: "The attack in daylight in the snow by B Coy in which I was then a corporal was designed as a diversion to a bombing raid up a support trench on our left. We were supposed to be supported by A Coy following on but they were withdrawn. We never got to grips with the enemy but were stopped in sight of them and had to "hole up" in craters and shell holes till nightfall and then got back to our original line. Casualties were very heavy. All officers killed or wounded and only one sergeant left and the Q.M.S. It was in fact pure murder and I was lucky to escape untouched....It was bitterly cold and we were easy targets against the snow and in daylight....I think the vivid memory of the occasion helped me when I painted the picture and provoked whatever intensity of feeling may be found in it."

198 Dwight Shepler, *Battle for Fox Green Beach*

The United States of America entered the First World War too late for a systematic coverage of the war to be undertaken by artists, although active publicity campaigns were organized in which they had a major role. In the Second World War, there were active combat art programs.

200/201 Pablo Picasso, *Guernica*

The progress of this famous painting was thoroughly documented by Dora Maar, Picasso's mistress at the time, who took a series of photographs of the picture in its various stages. Picasso's political opposition to General Franco had already been expressed in a series of prints entitled *The Dream and Lies of Franco*. The painter even took office under the Republic as the Director of the Prado, whose pictures were put into storage during the Civil War.

The sources of the picture are closely connected with themes of Picasso's private imagery, here given wider significance. The bull, not here a destroyer but an onlooker who sees the causes of disaster, is clearly linked with the artist's bullfighting and Minotaur themes. The romantic image of a terrified horse is immediately seen as a

symbol of fear, while the dismembered figure, the broken sword, and the anguished human figures recall the destructive course of a bombing in which 2,000 died. The painting of Guernica transformed Picasso's working life during the year in which it was done – he worked on numerous studies, and many separate sketches and drawings were made; his drawings of human heads, distraught with grief, are particularly notable.

210/211 Pieter Breughel, *The Triumph of Death*

In a last battle of humanity, horsemen form a *danse macabre* in a foreground that also includes a king, a cardinal, a peasant woman and a pilgrim. The middle ground includes a ditch in which peasants are encircled by the dead, while in the background can be seen ships and towns in flames. Men sentenced to death were placed on the high posts, at the right of the picture.

215 Otto Dix, *Flanders*

The landscape of the Western Front in the First World War was a devastating experience, to which artists responded with pain and anger. The romantic identification of landscape with tranquility or mystical unity with the world was totally denied by the blasphemy of shattered stumps of trees and fields full of craters. Even undulations of ground, as in Nash's *Hill 60* (see page 214) were not natural but caused by underground mining. Dix painted and etched a savage indictment of the scarred landscape and the inhumanities of war.

217 Graham Sutherland, *The City, A Fallen Liftshaft*

The distorted shapes of buildings destroyed touched a chord in Sutherland's English romantic imagination. He produced some memorable images, of which this is one.

218/219 Eugène Delacroix, *Massacre of Chios*

After seeing paintings by Constable, Delacroix repainted the background of this picture, heightening his palette. A rival called the picture the massacre of painting. But Delacroix was an innovator in technique and continued to experiment through his life. The division of tones in his painting was an example for the Impressionists. Delacroix did not only paint scenes of the pathos of war, but also contributed to a major scheme of battle scenes at Versailles, where the Gallery of Battles, of importance to French history (including York Town), was given more space than the Hall of Mirrors.

219 Anton von Werner, *Crown Prince Friedrich by the Corpse of General Douai at the Battle of Weissenburg*

The Crown Prince is dressed as an infantry officer, but wears the "Old Brandenburg" boots of a Cuirassier. His staff are in the blue undress frock coats (Überrock) of their appointments. One wears the aiguilettes of an aide de camp.

220/221 Charles Comfort, *Dead German on the Hitler Line*

The artist was with the First Canadian Infantry Division during the Italian campaign of 1943-5. At Pontecorvo on the fortifications known as the Adolf Hitler line, the artist only made pencil sketches in an area that had not been cleared of mines, leaving finished works like this until later.

224/225 Francisco Goya, *The Horrors of War*

It has been said of Goya that while other artists showed regret for the revolution, he was the revolution itself. His two paintings of the *Second of May* and the *Third of May* epitomize revolt against the Napoleonic invasion.

Almost none of the prints known later as *The Horrors of War* were published during the artist's lifetime. They are universally considered the most striking and important works of graphic art that condemn the folly of war.

226 Jacques Callot, *Execution Scene* from *Grandes Misères de la Guerre*

This inventive print maker and shrewd observer was at the top of his career in the series of prints known as the *Miseries of War*. A new sort of ground for his etching made well-bitten copper plates, producing clear images, a certainty. He brought the same sharp perception to war that had made his reputation in Italy as a recorder of actors and beggars.

240 Diego Velasquez, *The Surrender of Breda*

Like Rubens, Velasquez was a courtier of importance to whom diplomatic business was entrusted. He had traveled with Spinola, the successful besieger of Breda. He had personal knowledge on which to base his characterization of the general's magnanimity, but he had not visited the Netherlands, so that for the background he had to rely on an engraving. Other sources for elements of the picture have been distinguished, and the scene is paralleled by Calderon's drama *The Siege of Breda*. Nevertheless, what is exceptional about the picture is the synthesis and balance of the elements – color, drawing, the compositional unity centered on the symbol of the city's keys – profiled against a light background and suggesting allusions to success in the upright Spanish weapons contrasted with the disarray of the Dutch. There is a sense of calm resolution.

241 Anton von Werner, *Proclamation of the Kaiser*

The Kraiser and the Crown Prince are dressed as Prussian field marshals, as is Moltke. Bismarck is wearing the uniform of the Cuiraissier regiment of which he was a reserve officer. The soldier in the foreground is a trooper of the *Gardes du Corps*.

245   Laura Knight, *The Nuremberg Trial*

First row of defendants from the top: Goering, Hess, Ribbentrop, Keitel, Rosenberg, Frank, Frick, Streicher, Funk, Schacht. Second row, Doenitz, Raeder, von Schirach, Sauchel, Jodl, von Papen, Seyst-Inquart, Speer, von Neurath, Fritsche.

248   Peter Paul Rubens, *The Conclusion of Peace*

Marie de Medici is conducted to the altar of peace by Mercury; Innocence helps her forward; Fraud, Anger and Envy seek to prevent her. Peace puts out the flame of war.

Rubens maintained a large studio to enable him to carry out his numerous commissions; his applicants for positions as studio assistants confirm his extraordinary reputation – more than 100 wanted to work for him.

251   Franz Pforr, *Rudolf of Hapsburg's Entry into Basel*

This painting by a leading Nazarene artist exemplifies the need felt for paintings that recorded national history. The derivation of a style that leads, it has been said, to a "fairy tale atmosphere" in Pforr's work, was from both the German Renaissance and Italian painters like Raphael.

List of Illustrations

II
Outbreak

III
Heroes & Leaders

IV
Campaigns

V
Sieges

VI
Battles

VII
Armageddon

Acknowledgements

The Authors wish to thank the following for permission to reproduce the illustrations: Africana Museum, Johannesburg: 111. Altc Pinakothek, Munich: 159. Archiv für Kunst und Geschichte, Berlin: 54, 55, 59, 88 (top), 90, 102, 108 (top), 166, 180/181 (bottom), 225 (bottom), 242 (left), 251 (bottom), 254/255. Art Gallery of Ontario: 32. Bildarchiv Foto Marburg: 21, 213. Bildarchiv Preussischer Kulturbesitz: 36 (top and bottom), 40/41, 52/53 (top), 109 (bottom), 116 (top), 160 (bottom), 161, 192 (left), 215, 220/221 (top), 241 (top). British Library: 38 (top), 143, 146/147 (bottom), 230. Trustees of the British Museum: 51 (bottom). Canadian War Museum, National Museum of Man, National Museums of Canada: 104 (bottom), 124 (left), 124/125, 125 (right), 220/221 (bottom). Coldstream Guards, London: 191. The Cooper-Bridgeman Library Ltd.: 30, 42, 56 (bottom), 91, 110 (top), 159, 174 (bottom), 177, 187, 202, 210/211, 219 (right), 239 (right), 241 (bottom). Mary Evans Picture Library: 82/83, 92, 211 (right). Fitzwilliam Museum, Cambridge: 249 (bottom). Frans Halsmuseum, De Hallen: 34/35 (top). The Solomon R. Guggenheim Museum, New York: 35 (bottom). Sonia Halliday Photographs: 253 (right). Robert Harding Associates: 22 (bottom), 51 (bottom), 52 (left), 53 (bottom right), 85 (top), 104/105 (top), 109 (top), 111, 112, 113, 118 (bottom), 129 (bottom right), 134, 142, 152, 158, 160 (top), 175, 178 (top left), 179 (right), 184, 185 (bottom), 186, 187 (bottom), 188/189 (top), 191, 198/199, 200/201, 212 (right), 246. Heeresgeschichtliches Museum, Vienna: 134. H.R.M. Queen Elizabeth II: 37, 148. Historical Picture Service, Inc.: 33 (top), 106, 133, 144/145, 212 (left). Michael Holford Photographs: 20 (bottom), 79, 108 (bottom), 174 (top), 176. Imperial War Museum, London: 28 (bottom), 39, 62, 70, 72 (left), 115 (bottom right), 120, 122, 123 (bottom), 126, 127, 128/129, 130/131 (bottom), 130/131 (top), 131 (top), 132 (bottom), 164/165, 196/197, 199 (right), 214, 216, 217 (top), 221 (right), 222 (top), 245. Editions Robert Laffont, Paris: 23, 81 (right), 105 (top right), 105 (bottom right), 178/179 (bottom), 192/193 (top), 193 (bottom right), 223, 242/243. Maine Peace Action Committee: 217 (bottom). The Mansell Collection: 17 (bottom), 24 (top and bottom), 25, 29, 148, 149, 248. The Metropolitan Museum of Art, New York: 15, 195. Henry Moore: 132 (top). Musée National du Château de Versailles: 186, 187 (bottom). Musée du Louvre: 31, 61. Musées Nationaux, Paris: 31, 61. Museo del Prado, Madrid: 14. National Army Museum, London: 153, 190. Trustees, The National Gallery, London: 2, 12/13, 12 (left). The National Gallery of Canada, Ottawa: 86. National Maritime Museum: 113, 116 (bottom), 118 (top and bottom), 119, 181 (right), 238/239. National Portrait Gallery, London: 71 (left), 77 (left), 88 (bottom), 107 (bottom), 180/181 (top), 185 (top), 249 (top). Peter Newark's Western Americana: 74, 77 (right), 188 (bottom), 194 (top), 198 (left). Novosti Press Agency, London: 51 (top), 72 (right), 73 (left), 110 (bottom), 157 (bottom), 163, 244. Photo Bibliotheque Nationale, Paris: 121 (top left), 146 (top). Photographie Giraudon/S.P.A.D.E.M.: 26 (top left) 75, 84, 156/157 (top), 183 (right). Rijksmuseum-Stichting, Amsterdam: 112. Royal Ontario Museum, Toronto, Canada: 10/11, 20, 194 (bottom). SCALA/Editorial Photocolor Archives: 22 (top), 28 (top), 50/51, 73 (right), 85 (bottom), 89, 94, 117, 151, 182/183, 226/227, 240, 250. National Air and Space Museum, Smithsonian Institution: 121 (right). Snark International: 11 (right), 56 (top), 60, 78, 80/81, 83 (right), 103, 107 (top), 123 (top), 154/155 (top), 155 (bottom), 162, 218/219, 222 (bottom), 247 (left), 252/253. Spanish National Tourist Office: 19 (bottom). Staatliche Kunstsammlungen, Dresden: 33 (bottom). The Tate Gallery, London: 87, 114/115, 132 (top). Ullstein Bilderdienst: 227 (bottom), 228/229. Victoria and Albert Museum, Crown Copyright: 71 (right), 76, 79, 115 (top right), 224, 225, 226 (left). Trustees of the Wallace Collection: 251 (top). Werner Forman Archive: 19 (top), 26/27 (top and bottom), 150, 247 (right). Yale University Art Gallery: 58.

The Authors also wish to acknowledge the following for text excerpts: Lieutenant-Colonel Martin Lindsay, *So Few Got Through*, William Collins & Sons Co. Ltd.: 104. Desmond Flower and James Reeves, *The War 1939-45*, Cassell Ltd.: 128, 133, 164, 220. Matthew B. Ridgway, *Soldier: The Memoirs*, Greenwood Press Inc.: 198. G.M. Gilbert, *Nuremberg Diary*, Eyre & Spottiswoode (Publishers) Ltd.: 244.

Although every effort has been made to ensure that permissions for all material were obtained, those sources not formally acknowledged here will be included in all future editions of this book.

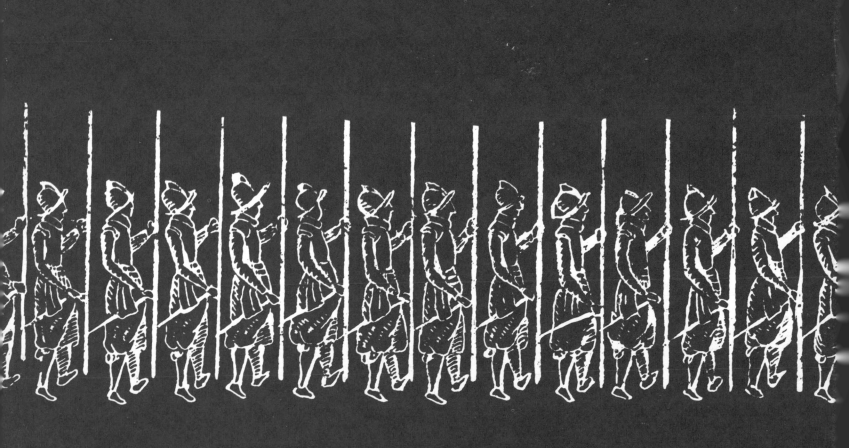